Your Map to Your Million

The Guide to Becoming a Millionaire in

Seven Years From $0.00

VMH

VMH Vikki M. Hankins™ Publishing
3355 Lenox Rd. NE Suite 750 Atlanta, GA 30326
www.vmhpublishing.com

Published in the United States by VMH Publishing.

Hardback ISBN: 978-1-947928-32-9
Paperback ISBN: 978-1-947928-33-6

10 9 8 7 6 5 4 3 2 1

Book Cover Design: Vikki Jones
Interior Layout: VMH Publishing
Book Cover Artwork: Shutterstock

Printed in the United States of America.

Contents

Foreward

My approach to this book is prayerful and cautious. I understand the influence that it could have on readers from all walks of life. My hope is that this book will inspire you, make you laugh, think, and cry, but most of all, guide you in your journey toward financial stability *and* your first million dollars. I want to provide the knowledge and tools to guide you as you create your map to your first million. But, it can be tough to take advice from someone you know nothing about. So, I wanted to take some time on the front end to let you know more about me.

I was born and raised in a small town in the middle of Mississippi in the late '60s. To be clear: that means no internet, cell phones, or 24-hour cable. I had very few examples of prosperity in my community. As a child, I would daydream just like other kids (and some adults) about being *rich*. Shows like *The Brady Bunch* and *Bewitched* offered me a glimpse into what life could be like. The stars of those shows lived in nice homes, had nice things, and money wasn't a major factor. Parents never fought about money. Kids didn't sneak money out of purses, or squirrel it away in coffee cans under their bed. The husband went to work, and everything in the household (besides the occasional comedic mishaps, of course) was comfortable and pleasant. This helped me adopt the mindset that if I worked hard and made plenty of money, I could become rich, like the people on television.

Fast forward 30 years later and you'll find me *below* broke. Wondering day-after-day, (which felt like minute-after-minute) *Where did I go so wrong?*

I wasn't lazy. I did what I had seen rich people do. I served my country by joining the military. I earned and received my college degree. I worked hard in a stable job, earning more than the average person. I was even able to buy some of those nice things I had seen sitting on Carol Brady's kitchen counter, and parked in Darrin Stephens' driveway.

Yet, I had nothing to show for it at my lowest point. After a multitude of bad relationships and a divorce, the little boy from Mississippi who wanted to be rich, was in the middle of his second (and, thankfully, final) divorce. It seemed like I went to sleep a young man, and woke up the next instant in my car in the parking lot at a local Walmart. During the separation, I didn't even have money for a hotel. My neck, back, and throat hurt, and my leg had gone numb. I only woke up because a bagger came to collect shopping carts, and the loose wheels and rattling metal baskets were loud enough to jar me out of my sleep. All this because my soon-to-be ex-wife was swinging and dancing like Ali throughout these divorce proceedings. We even owned rental properties together, and I couldn't stay there. Imagine having "ownership" of twenty warm, comfortable, dry bedrooms, yet you have nowhere to lay your head. In spite of the fact that I (and she) made decent salaries and owned property, we were still living paycheck-to-paycheck, because we lived so far above our means.

Showers only came from sneaking into gyms, pretending to use the exercise bike, lifting weights, or stretching, and then scurrying off to the locker room. I didn't have anywhere to cook a meal for myself— no stove or microwave.

At this abysmal point in my life, I woke up out of sleep again from those loud carts. I moved my truck one last time to not look so suspicious, but how many super loud shopping carts are there?! As I searched around my car, which was the home for my 30-ounce McDonald's bathroom cup— yes, bathroom cup, I watched the Walmart bagger pushing a column of carts back toward the front of the store. I decided then and there that I would obtain financial freedom, and become a self-made millionaire. Just like how I figured out how to survive without a house and bathroom, I would put a plan in motion that would push me from surviving, to living, and (eventually) thriving in my life. So, here we go.

Introduction

This how-to guide to become a millionaire in seven years is the perfect read for the person who desires this dream, but doesn't know where to begin. This book provides the reader with the knowledge, tools, and inspiration to become a millionaire. This is NOT a get rich quick scheme where you make someone else rich by selling a pipe dream, like those house flipping tours or pyramid schemes. Those schemes often require the sacrifice of your integrity with your friends and family, because they have to buy this "new product" that you pressured them to purchase. This book is a compilation of the most easily understandable principles, and it is also a real world guide to truly becoming a millionaire.

Have you ever been overwhelmed financially, while your already stretched budget was just wrecked by an unforeseen event, medical emergency, or even something as simple as a car repair? Have you ever wanted to be financially secure enough that money was not always the primary factor that controls your life? Well, *Your Map to Your Million* is the perfect book for you. In this book, you will learn the proven financial principles that every millionaire knows and practices. Your map to your million will start with a decision, because being wealthy is a decision. Without making a conscious decision to change your financial future, nothing will ever change. After you make the decision on where you want to go financially, you need to know where you are financially. The average person doesn't know their true financial reality of how much debt they are in, or how much in interest they pay monthly. This book will teach you how to get out of debt, and also teach you the principles of how money works. If you don't know how something works, then you can't fix it. Now, here is the exciting part, after learning some basic financial concepts, this book will guide you to financial stability, and your first million dollars in seven years. Imagine yourself enjoying, protecting, and maintaining your wealth, while living a debt free lifestyle.

I truly believe that success is not fully successful, until it is shared. I want to share with you the financial success I have attained, through exercising key financial principles. This is an opportunity to learn from my experiences, some good, and some not so good. I hope that my experiences will inspire you, inform you, make you think, provide guidance, and even make you laugh. Now, who wants to be a millionaire? Get ready to join our club. Welcome, fellow millionaire to be.

Chapter 1: The Decision

Overview

- You either make decisions, or have them made for you.

- Not making up your mind will only hold you back and make the journey to your first million take even longer, or worse, never come to fruition.

- Not every decision will give you the exact results you want, but you'll still have either made progress, learned something, or gotten what you needed, so it's **still** better than making no decision at all.

- Believing in yourself and your dream, and having confidence that you can achieve it, are essential to your success.

- Be mindful of how you talk about your goals; stay positive!

- Be aware of the people you keep around you. Steer clear of Dream Killers.

- Make a commitment to yourself, and your goals, that is free of doubt or hesitation.

13

I am starting this book with "The Decision" about making up your mind, because this was my first step to financial freedom. You think, why waste time on this, it's simple, just decide and do it! Well, it is not simple at all. Many people start an action without truly deciding to commit to their decision until the end. I always wanted to be wealthy, not just for myself, but more so to help the people that were in my life: my friends and family. I always started a financial endeavor, but sooner or later, I would get sidetracked by cars, trips, and expensive living, then I would slowly abandon my goal. I truly didn't make up my mind until one day while talking to my mother over the phone. My mother was complaining about her gas stove not working that well, and my dad wasn't moving fast enough in getting her a new one. We laughed over the phone, and in my heart I wanted to hang up the phone and have one delivered and installed that same day, but my wallet said that had to wait until Christmas. Well, time went on and I was still living life from day-to-day. I received a call from my dad one day, and that was extremely odd, because with Mom and Dad, Mom always initiated the calls, and Dad would hijack the phone, tell all the news, then give the phone back to Mom. Nonetheless, Dad called and said, "Timmy, how you doing," and at that point, I knew it was bad news. Dad proceeded to inform me that,

"Mother ain't doing so well." If you love your Mom like I do, then you know this frightens you. Dad said, "Don't worry, I think she is going to be ok."

Soon thereafter after talking with my Dad, I walked into the kitchen from cutting the grass outside in my home in Virginia. My wife approached me with tears in her eyes, and she said, "Your mom passed." At that very moment, everything stood still around me and my whole world changed with those three words. It was a tough night of crying, praying, and getting angry. I cried as I packed the car for the long journey home.

That next day, I traveled the seventeen-hour drive home, from Virginia to Mississippi, and it seemed never ending. After driving through the night, I arrived and walked into the kitchen through the front door, and there it stood in front of me: the old broken stove. At that moment, time stood still again, it was just me and that old broken stove. It was as if I had just heard the news of her passing all over again. That is why I decided to live my life financially stable, so I could help my friends and family around me. Don't let a broken stove in your life.

Make Up Your Mind

You can't achieve anything until you make up your mind. This is how your journey to your first million begins-- where the rubber meets the road.

Picture this: you're driving along the highway, headed to your favorite vacation spot for the summer. As you approach an exit ramp, you notice the car in front of you is deciding whether or not they're going to exit, or stay on the highway. They slow down, switch lanes, then switch back. Meanwhile, you and the other cars around you are stressed, and on high alert since you don't know what this car is going to do next. Some people honk their horns and scream at the person. Some people worry about the children or pets in their car. One car approaches behind the indecisive driver, but swerves at the last second and just barely avoids hitting them. The hesitant driver still hasn't made a decision at the last possible second, and finally just ends up crashing into the exit sign itself.

Have you ever seen people do things like that? They hem and haw until some outside circumstance or person makes a decision for them. They cause so much confusion and chaos, and end up making the people around them nervous and frustrated. This is exactly how financial decisions work. The longer you wait before making the decision of financial freedom, the more likely it is that somebody, or something other than you will do the deciding.

Making financial decisions can be described a lot like learning to swim. Most of the battle is simply with confidence. Confidence that you won't sink to the bottom, and confidence that, even if you DO sink, you have the skills to swim back to the top. When you can't believe either of these things, you panic, and you drown. When you believe both of these things, swimming is a relaxing, fun activity.

If you're an expert swimmer and someone drops you in the middle of the Atlantic Ocean, how much effort will you put forth in swimming to shore? The Atlantic is roughly 41.1 million square miles across. Half of that is 20.5 million square miles. Who in the world would think that they can swim that? When people look at their financial situation, it appears as vast as the Atlantic Ocean, and usually very little effort (if any) is given to getting closer to the shore. We believe, "I can't," instead of, "I'll find a way." We believe, "I'll never make it," instead of, "I'll just take it one mile at a time." This is how we defeat ourselves on a daily basis. We sit still when we could be swimming, and we complain when we could be making progress.

The first step toward becoming a millionaire is believing with everything in you that you will be successful.

The Power of Belief

The power of belief is one of the most influential tools that you will be using over the next seven years, until you reach your seven-figure goal, and join our Millionaire's Club. You can convince people of anything if you simply believe it in your own heart and mind first. This includes the fact that you can perform all the steps outlined in the book, and you can manage your financial habits in a healthier way. That's how you will meet your million-dollar goal within seven years. This isn't a time for, "Maybe," "I might," or, "We'll see." This is the time to be decisive and commit to the work you need to accomplish, so your finances will be where you want them.

The Power of Doubt

Doubt is just as powerful as belief. It can be paralyzing. However, the "great" thing about doubt: it is an internal obstacle. That means it is an obstacle where you have some level of control. There are already many external obstacles in your financial world that must be overcome, but holding onto an obstacle like doubt-- that you create and maintain of your own free will-- is pointless. It has no purpose at all but to keep you from achieving the goals that you want in life.

What's tricky about doubt, is that seeds of it are planted by other people, and even circumstances sometimes. When you fail at something repeatedly, seeds of doubt appear. When someone tells you that you can't do something, or that you'll never amount to anything of significance, seeds of doubt appear. However, even though the seeds may be there, you can choose not to plant them. Don't cover them in soil, water them, and give them sunlight to grow. Choose to throw those useless seeds right in the trash where they belong.

When we agree with our detractors, take failure as evidence of inadequacy (instead of just an opportunity to learn and grow), and pretend that we don't have what it takes to fulfill our dreams, then we are doing everything needed to help those seeds grow and snake through our spirit like life-sapping vines.

Getting Rid of Doubt

Understanding this much about doubt, you might be wondering how you can overcome the urge to fall victim to it. With most things in life, persistence is key. You get rid of doubt when you breed confidence. You breed confidence by being successful. You are more likely to be successful when you take your journey one simple step at a time.

Let's think back to the Atlantic Ocean swimming metaphor. If you decide to swim in place, and complain about the journey being too long, or hurting too much, then you will make no progress, and you will make yourself miserable. However, if you start doing some math and make a plan, then you can start getting yourself back home.

How many miles can I swim in a day? How many days should it take me to get back to shore? What items or skills do I have with me that will help make this journey faster, or less tiring?

These are the kinds of questions a confident person asks in an uncertain situation. They focus on solutions, instead of problems. They don't procrastinate and complain, they plan and execute. If you have tried to jump over a four-foot-tall wall and failed, then you might doubt that you'll clear the wall the next time you try. But, if you take time out to practice on smaller walls, then you can work your skills up to a point that a four-foot wall is no problem at all. By breaking the problem down into smaller pieces, taking the steps to prepare to reach the final goal, and believing that you will eventually be able to jump the four-foot wall, you end up being able to jump it with grace and ease.

The Power of Speech

You may have heard people say, "Speak it into existence." You said you hope it doesn't rain, and it does. You said you didn't feel like getting into a long conversation with your boss today, and you did. We tend to not give the power of speaking things aloud the credit that it deserves. Believe it or not, when we speak, we are not just speaking to another person in the room, we are speaking to ourselves. Believing is internal confidence in ourselves-- **knowing** that we can accomplish what we set out to. Positive speech is external confidence in ourselves-- **stating** that we can accomplish what we set out to do. The more you say something, the more it becomes your reality, for better or for worse.

Take note of the speech patterns you hear from other people. You will likely find that uptight, stressed, and frustrated people often have a lot of negative things to say, and a multitude of things to complain about. Yet, when you hear someone speak who seems to be doing okay in life-- financially or otherwise-- they'll often discuss positive things, be able to offer upbeat insights about various situations, and have a calm, or even sunny attitude. You might think at first the reason for this is because unpleasant people are just complaining about the random, terrible things that happen to them, and the pleasant people are calmer because random, good things happen to them for no reason. However, I'm going to ask you to reconsider that notion. What I've found (along with various studies on what's called the Law of Attraction) is that those people who have that positive, confident, "I'll figure out a way to make it work," attitude tend to **draw** beneficial circumstances, and people, to them. On the flip side, the negative, doubt-filled, "Everything sucks," crowd is actually drawing negative circumstances, and people, to them.

When you speak about your financial success, even if your finances are not **yet** where you want them, speak as if they are exactly how you want them. Don't be afraid to be cautious about who you share your financial planning with. There are negative, doubt-filled Dream Killers, all around us. Dream Killers do not see any value in your financial freedom (or even their own), and they are not willing to do what it takes to achieve that freedom. However, this also may manifest itself as them attempting to sabotage your journey to your financial goals. They may even overtly convince you that the task is too hard (*"You can't swim half the Atlantic!"*), or that the goal is too far away to reach.

I recommend that you surround yourself with financially prudent people, from whom you can also pick up some good money-management habits.

Committing to Yourself

One thing I always tell people around me is, if you don't make a decision for yourself, eventually, someone, or something, will decide it for you, and you probably won't like the results. Think about it like this: if you refuse to change your diet, and you are eating extremely unhealthy food (the kind you order from your car, or pour out of a box), then your doctor is going to eventually put you on a restrictive diet. You could ignore this, only to experience more severe consequences later. You might grow morbidly obese and develop diabetes, which could led to your foot being amputated and you spending the rest of your life wheelchair bound. Or it could result in you paying thousands of dollars for a prosthetic foot to replace the one you were born with. Were the burgers and cookies really worth it? I know this was overly dramatic, but you get the picture.

Take the time **now** to make the decision for yourself that will be most beneficial for you and your family. Don't be mistaken in thinking that there is such a thing as not deciding. Settling on "doing nothing" doesn't actually mean that nothing will ever be done about your financial situation. All it means is that you are giving up your power to choose. Deciding to place your financial life in the hands of others is never a good idea.

I suggest that you take this decision-making time to develop your map to your first million, and really reflect inward, and be honest with yourself. You must recognize the urgency of the need to change. In this early phase of the process, it is not important to decide exactly what you are going to do, but you must come to the conclusion that there is an immediate need to do something. This is the time to be your own adviser. Don't look at other people's situations, because no matter how much you know about a person's circumstances, it is impossible to know all the financial details involved.

One approach is to list the pros and cons of the two very distinct paths you must choose between: doing nothing (i.e., giving up your power), or acting now. Ask yourself, after you've completed the list, if you really want to do this. Especially think about whether or not you are willing to put in the work and make the sacrifices required to stick to it.

If you're still on-board to becoming a millionaire in seven years, follow me through the rest of these steps and let's get you set on the right path to make it happen.

Many times I try to convince people to take their financial life seriously, and that is very difficult, because they can't see the financial dangers ahead, but I can see them plain as day. It is similar to having a friend take a nap on a set of railroad tracks, and a train is coming around the bend. I can hear the train and feel the ground trembling, but my friend is comfortable taking their nap on the tracks. I try with urgency to convince them to get up from their comfort zone, because danger is coming. I realize that they can't hear or see the train as I do, and I keep trying to convince with passion. My friend, make your decision, you are on that track.

Another big decision to decide is if your desire is to truly be wealthy, or simply give the appearance of being wealthy. I know that doesn't seem to be much of a decision, however it is. Many people make an effort to appear more financially sound than they actually are. Buying luxury automobiles and designer clothes when you cannot afford them is dying a slow financial death. In today's society, there is pressure from all angles to give in to the over-hyped financial world. Faking it until you make it does not apply in the personal finance world. So much emphasis is placed on money and financial abundance, that people are treated differently if they appear wealthy, therefore it is tempting for someone to imply that they are financially powerful. People tend to keep financial matters very close to the vest, and individuals are usually more comfortable talking about their sex life more so than their financial life. Most people who wear a great deal of designer clothes and handbags are poor. They use those items to make themselves worthy and accepted. If you work a 9 to 5, and drive a $90,000 car, you are doing it wrong, unless you have already achieved financial freedom. Driving that big car to the company parking lot only indicates a high car payment.

A few years ago, I had a friend that was always getting put out of his apartment, and because I had a red pickup truck, he thought that I was U-Haul. So, about once a quarter, I would get the call that his stuff was put on the street again, and my personal U-Haul truck was needed to move the stuff to storage. My friend loved to dress nice in designer clothing, shoes, and had a full closet of designer attire. However, when you get thrown out, the movers don't take the time to pack your designer clothes neatly. They throw Nautica in a big trash bag, and I moved that trash bag of clothes probably ten times. Growing ever frustrated during one of the impromptu moves, I stopped him and did a little math. I took one of the trash bags full of clothing and took out one piece at a time, and then asked him how much he paid for each piece. He was very proud of the expensive items he adorned himself in, and was not ashamed to announce the price he just paid for those new FILAs. He remembered the price of each item well. Piece by piece, as I removed the items, he would shout out the amount that he paid, and I would put the amount in my calculator. After completing this exercise, the total amount paid in that one trash bag was $1,650.00, enough to pay his rent for two months. Also, there were still several other full bags of clothes. Thankfully, my friend got it together financially, but he still likes to dress nice. However, before we judge my friend so harshly, do the math on your closet, and see if you have more in your closet than your bank account.

MAP TO YOUR MILLION

Decision Making Exercise

You either make decisions or have them made for you. Not making a decision is actually making the decision that you are comfortable in your current situation. Be mindful of how you talk about your goals--stay positive! Make a commitment to yourself and your goals.

1. List two courses of action.

2. List positive consequences and negative consequences under each course of action.

3. Weigh your options and select the course that will benefit you the most.

4. Write out the course you decided to take, along with the consequences.

5. Create an extensive list of individuals and entities that have the ability to assist you with attaining the goal you decided (and leverage them).

6. Create an extensive list of individuals and entities that have the ability to hinder you with attaining the goal you decided (and avoid them).

7. Strategically communicate your course.

Chapter 2: Learn Your Financial Reality

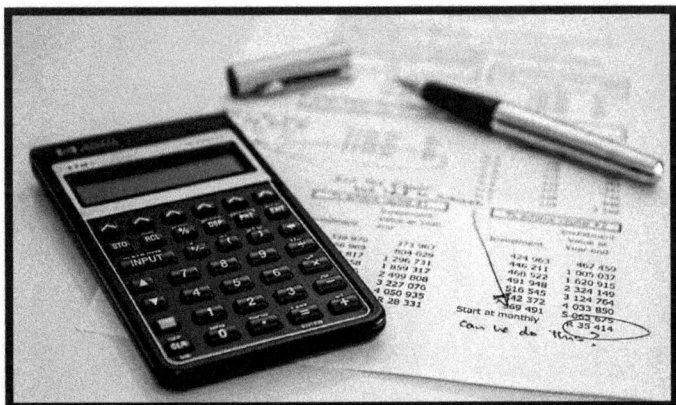

Overview

- (Key) Net worth = (Cash + Assets) - Debts.
- 401K Explained
- IRA Explained
- Unless you know what someone's debts are, then you don't know their true financial situation.
- Lots of people *look* rich, but very few actually are.
- Take an honest inventory of ALL of your debts, and ALL of your income.
- (Key) Connect with everyone you owe money to in order to negotiate more favorable terms for you (lower

interest rate, lower payments, more manageable payment methods for you, etc.).

- Create a plan of action to chip away at your debt as much as possible.
- Start thinking about ways that you could increase your income.

I find it amazing that there are so many people in the world who say they want to become millionaires, but very few have a clear road map outlining how they are going to arrive at that particular landmark.

One of the first things I ask people when I meet them (granted the conversation has something to do with money) is, "Can I see your map to your million?" Most often I get a response like, "What is a map to a million?" While I'm often sad and disappointed that they don't already have one, I'm also eager and happy to share my map with them. It's always pretty easy since I keep my map on my phone. But, I also keep copies on my desk, in my office, as well as in my kitchen and near my recliner at home.

When you finish developing your map, I encourage you to keep several copies around you in the places that you spend most of your time each day. These copies will serve as a constant reminder of what you are trying to accomplish and how you are going to accomplish it.

Now that you have made the commitment to yourself to see this journey through to the end, it's time for the rubber to meet the road. The first step towards action will be an assessment of your current situation. This is one of the most difficult steps in this entire process. Why? Most people do not want to know where they really stand. In other words they cannot handle the reality of their situation. Somewhere in the back of their mind, they have some idea that it's not going well-- especially when the bill collectors call--but they choose not to focus on it, lose track of the magnitude of their debt, and let it fester over time. They try to make themselves feel better with vacations, clothes, and other material things they can't really afford.

The worst thing to do in this world is lie to yourself. You cannot live in a world of delusion where you don't manage your problems, and instead give them free reign to eventually manage you. I call this "Lie-reality," living a lie. Sometimes we live in a lie-rality as a coping mechanism, because reality is just too terrifying or overwhelming for us to face ("Oh, no! I have to swim across half of the Atlantic!).

A common lie-rality I hear people talk about is that there is some magical financial bailout coming in our future. This could be something like a tax refund check, or bonuses that are being promised at work. Since we "know" this is coming, we decide that it's okay not to plan for our financial future, and to not treat our money with respect. Yet, when I talk to some of these people-- especially the ones with a pending lawsuit settlement-- they want me to give them money to get through "This little situation I'm in." Again, this book is about staying out of a "little situation."

Another way to think about it is this: You wouldn't promise your landlord you're going to pay your rent when you win the lottery next week, because there are many uncertainties that come along with such an arrangement. What happens if you don't win enough to pay your rent? What if the lottery system is dissolved before the next drawing? What if you lose your ticket? What if--and I know this is a stretch, but work with me-- you don't win **anything at all**?

If you do win, great. Use that money to make your dreams come true, but don't pretend you can depend on that money. Look for more reliable sources of income to plan with, including your income from your regular, full-time job, and your income from your possible side hustle.

What is a 401K? How Do You Start One?

401K receives its name from the Internal Revenue Code 401K. The code established a method in which eligible employees may make salary deferral (salary reduction) contributions on a before-tax, and/ or after-tax basis. Employers often make matching contributions over, and above, salaries negotiated. You start your 401K through your employer, and they set their own conditions and standards for you to participate in the program.

IRA Explained

An Individual Retirement Account is an investing tool used by individuals to earn and earmark funds for retirement savings. The most important part of the IRA, is the fact it's an INDIVIDUAL retirement account, established by that individual, for that individual. It differs from the 401K, because that is offered by your employer.

Honestly Calculate Your Net Worth

Net worth is the value of everything you own (assets), minus the value of all its outstanding liabilities. Think of it like this, if you had to sell everything that you own (home, car, clothes, etc.), and pay everyone that you owe, then the money you have left is your positive net worth. If you sold everything, and are unable to pay everybody that you owe, then that is considered a negative net worth.

An asset is a resource where an economic value can be determined above $0.00. In other words, anything of value that can be converted to cash! Most things can be considered either an asset or a liability, depending on the amount owed on it. Take a simple pair of shoes, if you buy those shoes on credit for $20.00, and you can easily sell those shoes for $25.00, then those shoes are an asset. However, if you can only get $15.00 for those same shoes, then those shoes are a liability. Liabilities are the amounts owed to creditors for previous services and merchandise.

During financial counseling, I ask the individual, "How much debt do you think you owe," and the dollar figure I receive is usually very wrong. Usually, they estimate a much lower number than it really is, and this could be for several different reasons, from miscalculations, embarrassment, or possibly too objective.

A common mistake I see is when people don't count certain debt as actual debt, for example: not counting student loans because they are deferred, or medical bills because they are not paying them. Those are two huge mistakes, because some student loans never go away and cannot be forgiven, even in bankruptcy. Also, federal student loans may be able to garnish some federal benefits, and the unpaid medical bills are killing your credit.

Actual situation: A young lady told me that she had a net worth of $230,000.00, and she made this assessment because she "owned" her own home with

50K equity. She stated she had $60,000.00 in her job 401K, she owned 2 Mercedes vehicles, and the one she had paid off was estimated the value at $20,000.00. She estimated her household goods and furnishings at a value of $85,000.00, and finally she estimated her jewelry at $15,000.00. People tend to drastically overestimate their assets and drastically underestimate their debts, and that is only hurting your situation. Honesty with yourself is critical.

Here was her actual situation. She overestimated her house value and didn't account for the usual 6% Realtor commission, repairs, and closing cost. She did have equity in her home, but it was roughly $18,000.00, not the 50K estimated. The 60K in the 401K was actually 56K, but that was not accessible without penalty. The paid off $20,000.00 Mercedes was drastically overestimated and needed repairs before it could be sold at market value of 12K, and luxury cars are expensive to repair. The liquidated Benz would net around $9,700.00, however, she was upside down on the new Benz $7,000.00, and owed more than the car was worth. Household goods and jewelry is always a diminishing return, as new styles come out in addition to wear and tear. If the average person had a yard sale and sold everything in the home, it would net around $7,000.00 on a good day. She also forgot to mention the

$38,000.00 in student loans, the $18,000.00 in credit card debt, and finally that $12,000.00 medical bill that was outstanding. Finally, after I deducted the $14,000.00 tax bill, and other miscellaneous debts that was due, her actual net worth was negative $300.00.

This scenario is dramatic, but very common.

In case it has never been explained to you, net worth isn't just how much money you have in the bank. Net worth refers to how much liquid cash (dollar bills) and assets you have, MINUS your debts. For example, if someone has purchased a $100,000 home, currently has a car worth $25,000, and $50,000 in the bank, then some people would say that they're worth $175,000. Not bad, right? But, in order to calculate their actual net worth, you must first subtract their debts from their total: $100,000 in mortgage debt, $25,000 in unpaid credit card bills, $50,000 on a home-equity line of credit they took out last year, and $50,000 in unpaid tuition for their children who are in private school. That's $225,000 in liabilities. Now their financial reality looks a little different.

$175,000 (assets) - $225,000 (liabilities) = $-50,000 (net worth)

This is why I said you can't look at the surface

of someone's situation to truly know what's going on with them. All that glitters is not gold. Even though it may look like everything is going well on the outside (house paid off, kids in private school, $100,000 in cosmetic surgery), if you have no debts and $5 in your pocket, then you have a higher net worth than this person!

In this economy, even one million dollars is not the end all be all. But that's okay. If you absorb and apply the principles outlined in this book, then you will have a foundation for building wealth that goes above and beyond a single million dollars. Obtaining a million dollars is simply a small piece of adopting a wealth-building lifestyle for the rest of your life.

Becoming a millionaire is not some distant, unattainable goal, even though people often speak about it as if it's on another planet. Becoming a millionaire is actually quite easy and fun once you know the precise steps to take.

Imagine how hard being an electrician without the proper education would be. Understanding the basic principles of electromagnetism and electrodynamics is crucial. If you started attempting to help people with their appliances and electrical wiring without proper training and education, then you'd be in for a shocking experience, to say the least, and might even end up killing yourself.

The same idea applies when referring to money. You could cause yourself serious financial hardship, or death, (a.k.a. 'broke') if you don't understand the basic principles of how money works, and how to manage it properly.

Method Over Madness

There is a huge difference between methodically mapping your way to a million dollars, and making a lot of money that subsequently adds up to a million dollars. Mapping your way to a million is deliberate, careful, and sustainable, because it is planned and managed. Making a lot of money--maybe even a million dollars--is haphazard, chaotic, and fleeting. Why do you think that there are celebrities like MC Hammer and Mike Tyson (sorry, Mike. We still cool, right?) who seem to be on top of the world financially, professionally, and socially, and then the next thing you know you're hearing about them being homeless, going to court for trying to not pay taxes, or filing for bankruptcy? They had well over a million dollars coming in every single year, but they didn't deliberately and carefully manage each and every dollar that came their way. As bystanders, we often exclaim, "That's a shame," or "All that money and ain't done nothin' with it," or similar phrases.

At the same time, we do that exact same thing, even though we haven't gotten millions of dollars in lump sums before. Think about it. How long have you been a part of the workforce? You work forty hours or more every week for years on end, and what do you have to show for it? Are you still thousands of dollars in student loan debt? Are you still regularly using credit cards instead of paying for things directly? Do you own any property yet, or are you still renting? So, Kettle, let's not be so critical of Pot, shall we?

Sometimes the truth hurts, but that doesn't mean you don't deal with it. You can't defend yourself against an enemy that you can't face.

Get Rich Slowly

People tend to temporarily lose all ability to make sound judgments when they get large sums of money at one time (such as a tax refund check or winning money at a casino), my recommendation is that you focus on getting rich slowly.

Any time you run into someone who exclaims that you can get rich quick, don't walk, **run away**! That isn't an impossible task, but trying to sell random, questionable products online, or guessing which stock will be worth ten times its current value in a week is usually not the best use of your time when you're trying to reach your million-dollar goal. Not because the money wouldn't be just as green, but because these outcomes are highly unlikely to make you any profit.

I once had someone try to talk me into selling $29.99 teeth whitening kits. They claimed they would support me, help sell them, and that I would get rich, like some other people they heard got rich (no one that they had ever met in person or talked to, apparently). Keep in mind that this person was in no manner affiliated with the profession of dentistry--not a dentist, not a dental hygienist, not even a receptionist at a dentist office! The drive behind their scheme was a desire to get a lot of money quickly (without thinking things through). I did the math on their "plan." If they made a 50% profit on each kit sale, a million dollars was 66,666 kits away (and I don't even like the number 6 like that). Keep in mind that does not factor in how much it might cost to advertise online, print flyers, drive to conventions or fairs, rent a booth or table, or store and buy more kits. The point is, that hasty idea was designed to fail.

You're free to waste your money on these kinds of ventures if you'd like, but I'm encouraging you to create and stick with a solid plan. Your map will be a concrete set of steps that you will follow based on your own goals and circumstances, not some get rich quick scheme that someone thought up to try and trick honest, hard-working people out of the little money that they have.

The only way to get rich quick, is by starting a get rich quick scheme! No! Stop right there. The term "get rich quick" has been used to describe shady investments since at least the early 1900s. Think about it for a second. Do you really know anyone who has obtained wealth via a successful get rich quick scheme? Most get rich quick schemers do portray that high society, but they leave out the fact that they received that lifestyle by tricking others to invest in a failing idea. I go to those "house flipping" seminars all the time for fun, and see up close and personal someone being taken by a get rich scheme. The last one I went to, the salesperson was like a preacher, and it was as if we were in church. He took us on an emotional roller-coaster, and within 90 minutes he had a line of people lined up in the back of the ballroom who had limited resources already, ready to commit those last resources (sometimes thousands of dollars) to an idea they just sold on. They took cash, credit cards, and even IOUs. Those IOUs were legally binding, and would show up on your credit report if you didn't pay. The presenter was so smooth when he slipped in that little fact by saying, "We are even going to help build up your credit, isn't that great?!" In my head when I heard that, I thought, *What?!* I often attempt to warn people at these events, but I usually get labeled a Dream Killer. The presenters fulfill their due diligence by pre-warning the audience not to listen to people trying to talk them out of this opportunity. Well, let me be the first to tell you that I have been in real-estate investing for years, and you pretty much meet all the investors in your area, because you're doing the same thing and sharing the same ideas and resources. I was talking to one of the Real Estate seminar staff members as I was leaving the ballroom and asked about their schedule. He informed me they go directly from city-to-city during the entire year, except 3 weeks for holidays. So when do they have time to flip those houses?

Hand-to-Mouth Curse

Even if you've never actually heard of this dreaded predicament before, chances are you've seen someone suffer the symptoms of it. The hand-to-mouth (H2M) curse is the worst financial condition. The H2M curse is as a way of life in which you hardly have enough food or money to live. However, the worst thing about H2M is that you are unable to do anything for anyone else. H2M sufferers are always looking for their next source of money or provisions. H2M sufferers often live with others, or with substantial government assistance. They even receive substantial free government assistance, and even then they are usually still unable to make their basic ends meet. You will periodically receive a text, instant message, or email with a description of circumstances that the H2M sufferer experiences. Only to be followed up with a request for financial assistance. The H2M sufferer has a keen sense of how to play on emotions and they have little to no dignity of their request for assistance.

This is definitely not to make fun of or put anyone down, but simply to make aware, and I didn't want to sugarcoat it before I served it up. Getting that as direct as possible is extremely important, because every one of my trainees or clients who recognize and accept the fact that they are living from hand-to-mouth, made a drastic turn around, and now are some of my favorite success stories. They realize how difficult hand-to-mouth living is and figure out how money works, then they begin loaning instead of borrowing, and working their map to their million with ease.

Symptoms of the H2M Sufferer

- Has no long term investments established.
- Can't nearly afford the lifestyle that they portray.
- Don't have any money at the end of the month.
- Invest more on entertainment than in an IRA.
- Does not know what the acronym IRA stands for.
- Messages on Facebook: "Will anybody let me and DaDa come live with them?" (actual message).
- "Borrows money" and never returns the loan.
- Have many color coded outfits with several selfies to document them, however a little challenged on rent money.
- Their phone has a better plan than them.
- Will give you the cold shoulder if/when you stop the endless giving.
- Always wanting top shelf expensive drinks at the bar.
- Very familiar with all the expensive restaurants in various cities.
- Quick to say that they don't have money, and quick to ask for it.
- Doesn't care about others situations, as long as their own needs are met.

But I Have Good News, the Hand-To-Mouth Curse Has a Cure!

The cure is, stop looking for what others have, or what they can do for you. Inventory your own skills and abilities. Make a plan and stick to it. Review the things that got you in this financial state, and stop repeating them. Set small goals and achieve them.

"Designed to Win" or "Designed to Fail"

How much money have you made over your lifetime? Where is it now? How much can you physically and fiscally put your hands on, or leverage? If your answer is very little, or none, then you are doing it wrong. From this day forward, you must establish passive income methods that can be leveraged the rest of your life. Passive income is income resulting from cash flow received on a regular basis, and it requires minimal effort from the recipient to earn it. Some passive income examples are: rents from an investment property, royalties from a book written, or song. Passive income is further defined in the IRS Publication 925. If every year you pledge to create diversified methods to generate $200.00 per month in passive income, then in ten years, you would have $2,000.00. Now, I understand that is not "make it rain" rapper money, but it sure takes the edge off from starting from nothing every month. The more passive income that you create every month, the better this method works. Passive income is King and can be calculated in your net worth. According to my method, you can count passive income as cash as long as that passive income is not temporary, based on a 6% return. For example, take $100,000.00 x .06 = $6,000.00 annually, and that is $500.00 per month. Therefore, in reverse, you can calculate $500.00 monthly passive income as having $100,000.00 in the bank. However, you can't have all your million in passive income. You can't get away that easy. The max you can calculate in your map to your million is 20%.

Examples of Passive Income that is Countable:

Military retirement pensions

Employee pensions

Social security benefits for retirement

Annuities

Rental income

Examples of Passive Income that is NOT Countable:

Welfare

Child support

Food Stamps

Unemployment Benefits

Passive Income to Cash Chart	
Monthly Massive Income Amount	Dollar Equivalent
$500.00	$100,000.00
$1000.00	$200,000.00
$1500.00	$200,000.00
$1500.00	$200,000.00

The max you can calculate in your map to your million is 20% or 200K.

Myth of Home Ownership

I hear many people refer to themselves as a "homeowner." However, if ABC Bank loaned you the money to purchase the home, then the actual homeowner is ABC Bank. You're only to maintain their interest and pay taxes. Interest is very confusing to most consumers, but if you think of it this way, it makes it much clearer: interest is the cost of borrowing money. You pay interest to borrow money, and you get paid to loan money. The interest rate depends on how expensive it is to borrow the money. The higher the rate, the more expensive it is. For example, if you borrow $100.00 at an annual interest rate of 10%, at the end of the year, you'll owe $110.00. If you loan $100.00 at an annual interest rate of 10%, at the end of the year, you will have $110.00. Compound interest is as simple as earning interest on the money you earned in interest.

An associate of mine once asked me what title I would give before "homeowner," and without thinking about it, the first thought that popped in my mind was "sucker." You may think that is pretty harsh, but if you think about what actually takes place, it is actually a win, win, win, win situation for ABC Bank. The first win for ABC Bank is they have a guaranteed asset that is appreciating in value, and they will always be aware of how to locate it. You can't hide or move a house in the middle of the night. The second win for ABC Bank is they collect mostly interest in the beginning of the loan, and even if you get smart later on and decide to stop the interest bleeding, they already have collected a majority of their money. There are several wins for the bank, but the final win I want to point out is you become the sucker, because you are taking great care of someone else's asset. Only to miss a few payments and receive an eviction notice. Next is the real Okie-doke, for simplicity sake, let's analyze a $1,000.00 (principal to interest) payment in year 1 and year 30 of a 30 year mortgage loan. Year one, ABC Bank would take $800.00 in interest payment, and only apply $200.00 towards the principal balance. In contrast to year 30 (if you last that long), they have officially got all the blood out of that turnip, and then apply $200.00 towards interest, and $800.00 towards your principal balance. I personally do not think that is a fair system. One little Tim Fact that I want you to remember is that you rarely attain home equity from paying down your mortgage. You gain a majority of your equity from value appreciation. For example, if you purchase 1 home for 100K and in 5 years you desire to sell it, you may have only paid down the mortgage by 5K, however the house value may have increased by 15K in those same 5 years. Therefore, it is more important when shopping for your home to look for homes in areas where homes are appreciating in value, not just the largest and shiniest homes. Always remember: location, location, location. Homes located in better school districts have a greater potential to grow in value. You do not truly own your home until you have retired the mortgage.

Look for updates on home buying on my website www.maptoyourmillion.com, and subscribe to have a one-on-one conversation with me on tips for home buying that is directly tailored to you.

The Importance of Decreasing Your Mortgage

For most Americans, their home purchase is their biggest investment, or asset. Therefore, it is important to maximize the investment potential. You do this by paying a little more each month on the principle balance. Mortgages are structured in a way that the mortgage company collects more interest in the beginning of your mortgage, when you are a new homeowner. By the time the kids are grown, you have moved up in your career, and can afford to make extra payments, the mortgage company welcomes that, because they have already squeezed all the blood from that turnip. Paying extra payments on mortgages is much less effective in years 15-30, than it is in years 1-15. The earlier the better. You can get all the benefits of an early payoff without the extra costs of a refinance by paying one extra payment per year. However, ensure you specifically tell the mortgage company the money is to be applied to the principal only. Principle is the amount that you borrowed for the home, minus any interest, taxes, and insurance. Most mortgage companies are directed, by default, to apply all extra money to the next mortgage payment due, which is a total benefit to them.

Another method is a bi-weekly plan where half the scheduled monthly payment is made every two weeks. A bi-weekly plan results in two more payments being made annually. In other words, under bi-weekly plans, 26 half payments are made annually, resulting in 13 full payments. This is recommended when you get paid on the same schedule. However, you must be very clear with your mortgage company of your intent, and I would recommend getting it in writing, or at least keep a detailed log of conversations to refer back to.

And finally, if possible, get a 15-year mortgage, if you can afford it. A 15-year mortgage usually translates into a lower interest rate, and is a lower risk to the bank. However, there will be a higher monthly payment. The result is much less interest paid to the bank, and you pay your home off in half the time of a traditional 30-year option. The drawback is, once you commit to a 15-year plan, you are liable for that payment amount.

Start with the lowest rate that you can possibly negotiate, and be careful of new mortgage products that come and go. These new products are developed in boardrooms; they are not meant to be helpful by putting money back in the hands of homeowners. But, you are going to need extra money applied to the principle.

Here are some recommendations and ideas for you to possibly adopt to pay off your home.

Annual yard sale

We have so much extra stuff that we accumulate over a year, and most of it sits around collecting dust, until it is not worth anything to sell. Perfect example, I ran out and purchased one of those voice command boxes that can turn on and off the lights, and play music. I paid full retail price for it a few years ago, and I used it for about 3 months, and have not used it since. Be aggressive in the yard sale, and put every dollar to work killing interest.

Tax refunds

Tax refunds should be applied to mortgage. Don't use this money as a vacation fund, or splurge on one of those voice command boxes that I bought. This is a very effective method to aggressively pay off your home. Depending how aggressive you are in 15 years, you can own your home debt free!

Give Uber a Try

No, don't call an Uber, drive one. Make a mortgage payment, and then stop!

Owning your home outright gives a person great sense of security, even though you can probably earn higher yields in other money markets, but the peace of mind is priceless. Even if you don't pay the whole thing off, you can pay down enough to request a re-amortization, and that could be the difference from a $3,000.00 payment, to a $550.00 payment, which would you rather pay each month?

Determining What Method Works Best for You in Creating Passive Income

Let me start by simply naming a few methods, because I know that some of you are drawing a blank. The easiest method is rental property, however it is the most used and abused. Here are more methods:

1. Rental property.

2. Your own home. If you reduce the amount of mortgage that you pay, it will net you the same amount.

3. Tax Liens. A tax lien is a lien imposed by law upon a property, to secure the payment of taxes. A tax lien may be imposed for delinquent taxes owed on real property or personal property, or as a result of failure to pay income or other taxes. These liens are auctioned off monthly to the public to the highest bidder on the city courthouse steps. Tax liens are such an attractive investment, because they usually pay very high interest rates of return on your investment. I have seen as high as 20% interest on return. If you loan $100.00 at an annual interest rate of 20%, at the end of the year, you will have $120.00. That doesn't appear to be much, but let's make that $100,000.00. If you invest $100,000.00 at an annual interest rate of 20% percent, at the end of the year, you will have $120,000.00. Not bad for one morning at the courthouse. This is also an example of passive income. However, be careful with any investments, because each city and state have different rules and regulations. Please seek professional advice before beginning this process.

4. Write a book, they never go out of style, and it's a great source of income.

5. Pensions. A pension is a fund into which a sum of money is added during an employee's (earning) years. From that fund, payments are drawn to support the person's retirement (rewarding years), in the form of periodic payments.

6. Franchising and branding.

7. Write a song.

8. Sing a song.

9. Plain old interest.

10.Cattle, trees, land.

Passive Income Exercise

The possibilities are infinite but the key thing is diversification. Here is an exercise that you can complete, to help you generate passive income:

1. Write a list of ten ideas that can generate passive income.

2. Associate an amount that you could potentially generate as a monthly passive (estimate low).

3. Write a schedule that you can dedicate to those activities.

4. Set a clear attainable goal.

5. Set a start date.

Chapter 3: Getting to Zero: $0.00

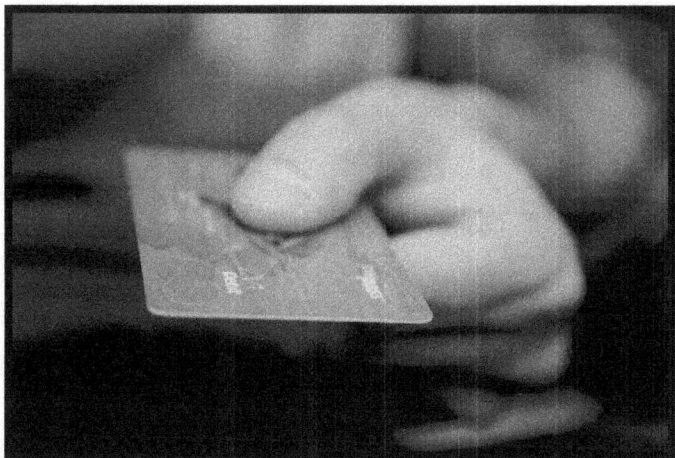

Overview

- You can't start your path to being a millionaire if you're drowning in debt.

- You first need to dig yourself out of the financial pit you're in so that you can reach the surface and start building wealth.

- Getting to a net worth of $0.00 is the first step toward becoming a millionaire.

I was standing at the gas pump on payday, in midsummer, 1998, gas on empty, driving a V-8 Ford Expedition GG (Gas Guzzler). I had been riding on fumes for some time, so I had no wiggle room. In fact, I did the old swerve trick to get to the gas station (if you don't know what the gas swerve trick is, then you've never been really broke). I inserted my debit card in the pump, lifted the handle, inserted it in the tank, and pulled the trigger, and nothing. What! There must have been some kind of mistake, it's payday! So, I re-inserted my card, and again nothing. So there I was, twenty plus miles from home, no gas, no money, all credit cards maxed, and it was record heat at 101 degrees. I called my now ex-wife, who was the money manager of the house, and it took 2 hours and 29 attempted calls to ask her what was going on. She told me she didn't know. Luckily, I saw some of my co-workers, and they loaned me gas money to get home. When I got home, I looked into the checking account and discovered we were paying last month's bills. We had gotten behind by 30 days. Even thought it was payday, we were in debt and spent more than what we were earning. I am definitely not blaming her, she was only doing what she thought was best, but I had no oversight over my own financial situation. I sat down in the living room, listed all my creditors, and came up with a plan to get out of debt. I soon realized that I let things go too far. The bills were getting paid by my wife, I had my allowance money, and I was happy. I trusted too many people. Bear in mind, it is ok to trust others, but when you trust, verify. Everyone must take responsibility and monitor their own individual health, and situation. Once you are in financial trouble, or debt, blaming someone else does nothing to help fix the situation. I recommend to leverage today's technology to monitor your own financial situation. The financial industry has created an abundance of tools, so the consumer can be informed.

Avoid Credit Card Debt Like It's the Plague!

When it comes to your financial life, minimum payments on your credit cards is the biggest trap in the business. Let's take a $2,000 credit debt with an 18% annual interest rate. A minimum payment of 2% of the balance, or $10, whichever is greater, would take 370 months or, just over 30 years to pay off. You are paying back more than double and triple of what they advanced you. I challenge you to go around your home and locate 30% of the items you purchased with that credit card. You can't! Usually, you are still paying for something that you either got too big for, or maybe it went out of style three seasons ago, or it just doesn't work anymore.

Remember that interest can work for you, or against you. It works against you when you borrow money, and works for you when you invest, especially when the interest compounds. "Compound interest (or compounding interest) is interest calculated on the initial principal and also on the accumulated interest of previous periods of a deposit or loan" (*Investopedia*). It is the result of reinvesting interest, rather than paying it out, so that interest in the next period is then earned on the principal sum, plus previously accumulated interest. Compound interest is standard in finance and economics. Simple interest is calculated only on the principal amount, or on that portion of the principal amount that remains. It excludes the effect of compounding. Simple interest can be applied over a time period other than a year, e.g., every month. The key here is, interest works against you in a bad way if you are in debt, or in borrowing. In fact, it is highly unlikely that anyone would be millionaires without interest. Wealth is constantly moving through society from one group, or person, to another. The old saying "The rich get richer, and poor get poorer" has some validity. Banks lend money, and they receive payments from the borrower. Usually, there is a fee for even requesting to borrow the money (funding fees), and if you are late on one of those payments, you are levied more money (late fee). On top of all of that, they get interest on all of it as well.

Living Below Your Means

Living below your means and investing the difference is one of the key principals I want you to take away from this book. It is impossible to get out of debt until you adopt this lifestyle. Many people hesitate to adopt this principle because of fear of being deprived. I will be the first to inform you that it is not a deprived lifestyle, and it is not permanent. I lived so far above my means years ago, and when I decided to become a millionaire, I adopted the lifestyle of living below my means. I remember my first own place after my divorce. After sleeping in motels, in my car, and wherever I could crash, this tiny condo was a huge welcome. The little condo was filled with filthy 30-year-old forest green carpet, busted toilets, and a wire clothes hanger nailed to the wall, functioning as a toilet paper holder. The ceiling and walls were so dirty that you really couldn't tell what the original color was. However, the worst thing was the smell, it was not of this earth.

With all that said, I was more excited about that place than the 1.6-million-dollar home I just moved from. It really hurt my feelings when I invited a close friend over to share in my joy, and after walking in for a few seconds, they turned and looked at me and said, "If this is where you are going to live, you don't have to worry about me coming to see you." Well, I purchased the place at a severe discount due to its condition, and moved in. I ripped up that filthy carpet piece by piece and carried it to the dumpster. As I rolled the carpet and threw it on my shoulders to carry, the dirt from the carpet turned to mud as it touched my face. I dealt with the disgusting odor and heat as they battled to see which one was to knock me out first. I also dealt with waiting on the police response of the possible blood stains I found on the floor underneath the carpet, which turned out to be non-human blood.

At first it was tough, however, I look back at the struggle and it was totally worth it! I was able to pay the condo off in a matter of months, and I lived there comfortably as I recovered financially. I was able to renovate the place while I lived there, and by the time I was finished, I had a snazzy little place where people would ask for a tour when they visited. Even my buddy who indicated that I would never receive a visit from them was a frequent visitor. Now, years later, this is one of many very profitable investments that provides me wealth in equity, passive income monthly, and keeps gaining in value as an investment.

Every time you make a decision that is below your means, you will more than likely receive a greater financial benefit. So, skip the BMW and get the Chevy, skip the expensive seafood restaurant and go to the farmer's market, skip the tailored suit spot and go to GW Fashion (aka. Goodwill), and you will see an increase in your financial freedom. Make the decision today to start living below your means and investing the difference.

Your Credit Report is Your Word Report

This is due to the fact that a borrower asks for money, and gives their word that they will repay. The lender uses this tool as a report card to see if you keep your word with other lenders, to determine how well you keep your promise of repayment. Credit is the access of money, and will be an important factor to use strategically in your map to your million. Too much credit can be detrimental, but the access to credit is very beneficial. Therefore, your credit should be monitored and maintained.

What is good credit? Good credit is a FICO score between 690 and 720. A FICO score can range between 300 and 850. Your credit report has 5 major categories and they are: Payment History (35%), Debt Burden (30%), Length of History (15%), Types of Credit (10%), and Recent Credit Searches (10%). Changing those 5 major categories is the ONLY way to "fix" your credit. One of the benefits I want readers to take away is this key fact: "credit repair" companies cannot raise your credit score. The only thing they can do is challenge incorrect items listed on your credit. The scam is, they challenge everything on your credit in the hopes the creditor stops reporting the negative items on your credit, therefore temporarily increasing your credit score. However, this is rarely successful due to the three major credit reporters catching on. Now there are limits that determine the rate at which your credit score can go up or down each month. So, on your journey to your million, don't use the "credit repair pros" that will charge/ scam you anywhere from 300-800 dollars. Simply make payments on time, reduce your amount of debt, and reduce the number of credit searches. Finally, don't be reluctant to ask your creditors to change their negative reports after you have paid a predetermined amount of payments on time. Your creditors will in most situations, as long as you keep your word to repay according to the agreement.

Poor credit-- FICO score under 630
Average-- FICO score between 630 and 690
Good credit-- FICO score between 690 and 720
Excellent credit-- FICO score above 720

I developed a plan to get out of debt in 18 months. I monitored my plan daily and called my creditors daily. In fact, one of my maxed out credit cards was just in my spouse's name, and I was only an authorized user. When I called them, they had to get permission from my wife to speak about the account. She wasn't home and didn't answer her cell phone, so I called them back and said she was here and had given permission to discuss the account. The company asked to speak to her, and in my brilliant plan, I changed my voice to sound like a woman (didn't work), and in my man/lady voice, I said, "I give permission to discuss the account." The customer service representative said, "Mr. Jernigan!" I immediately hung up the phone.

I hope the customer service representative I was speaking to doesn't buy my book. However, I pressed forward and kept communicating to my creditors. I first estimated being debt free in 18 months, but instead, I was debt free in 9.

Not being able to speak financially confidently was a depressing feeling. I couldn't help my loved ones in the way I wanted to while in debt. You can't start your path to being a millionaire if you're drowning in debt. You first need to dig yourself out of the financial pit you're in so that you can reach the surface and start building wealth.

Getting to a Net Worth of $0.00 is the Initial Step Toward Becoming a Millionaire

Getting to 0 simply means attaining a debt free lifestyle. Interest and penalties are hidden very well by creditors, and are now being accepted by consumers as the norm. Let me be the first to let you know, if you have excessive debt, then you are doing it wrong. In every financial article or presentation, I discuss debt and how to reduce it. It is sometimes difficult in today's society to completely get rid of debt, but minimize it as much as possible. All debt is not bad. Good debt is debt where you earn more than the money cost. For example, a home where the value is increasing more than the money cost to borrow, is a good debt. You earn a high return on investment (ROI). ROI stands for Return On Investment, it is the amount of money that is returned back to the investor, minus the initial investment. If you invest $100,000.00 at an annual interest rate of 20% percent, at the end of the year, you will have $120,000.00. In this example, the return on the investment is $20,000. Bad debt, most debt fits in this category, like credit cards, and consumer loans, is where you get a low ROI. Consumer loans are simply any form of borrowing money for use of the consumer, and can be in secured or unsecured forms. The higher the risk, meaning the risk of the consumer not paying the loan back, the higher the cost of the loan.

Debt costs money! The average person is clueless about the actual amount of interest they are paying each month. Interest is simply the price you pay for being in debt. The average person throws away in interest over $500 a month for mortgage, over $100 a month in car financing, over $200 a month in credit cards, and another $150 in consumer loans. That's nearly a $1,000.00 a month. Your creditors own you. If you are indebted to someone, or something, you become dependent on that person, or entity.

You can't get ahead from behind. The benefits of living a debt free: lifestyle is stable, credit score goes up, and your stress level comes down. Family training and traditions are also developed: parents in debt usually have kids in debt, so it should encourage you to break the cycle. You increase your financial stability and become the lender, not the borrower.

Tim's Tips on Debt Free Lifestyle

1. Know where you are. When I was making my getting to zero plan, I asked my ex-wife for a list of all the bills, and I would only get a partial list.

2. Make a plan: make a list, check it twenty times:

   • High interest first.

   • High payment first.

   • Low balance first.

   • All options are ok as long as you use the snowball approach: use the money that you use to pay off one debt to the next debt. Say you pay off a store credit bill that is $65.00, then apply that extra $65.00 you have next month to the next debt you are paying off. This speeds up the process of paying off your debts, and is called snowballing.

3. Communicate, communicate, communicate:

   • With your creditors

   • With your family

   • With everyone-- people that you hang out with, who don't tempt you with a frivolous trip or event.

4. You can't borrow your way out of debt. Bill consolidation loans are ok to reduce your interest, but they are dangerous, because they usually stretch out

the terms. More often than not, the borrower goes out and attains more debt.

5. No outrageous goals!

- Setting goals too high will set you up for failure.

- The purpose of the goals are to be accurate.

6. Build a safety net. You don't want to get side tracked with unexpected expenses.

7. Increase income.

- Side hustle money goes directly to debt reduction.

8. Lower your responsibility.

- Cut cable.

- Negotiate better deals. Even your car and homeowner's insurance should decrease, but only if you call your insurance company and set up a meeting.

- Sell clutter.

9. Drop expensive habits.

- Bar nights.

- Shopping.

- Eating out at restaurants.

10. Monitor your credit.

- Check for accuracy.

11. Leverage technology.

- Banking apps.

- Credit score apps.

12. Recalculate your plan periodically.

- You will be surprised at your new financial swagger.

- Increase bargaining power.

13. Stick to it.

- Even when you get to 0.

- The same principals you used to get to 0, you will use the same principals to get to 1,000,000.

- You may have made the greatest financial shift in your life so far.

You can't start your path to being a millionaire if you're drowning in debt. You first need to dig yourself out of the financial quicksand, so that you can reach the surface and start building wealth. After getting to $0.00, you will keep using the same principles and lifestyle changes used to get out of debt, and start building wealth. Now, after you get out of debt, you will have more financial power. By living debt free, you become more financially powerful each day.

Chapter 4: What's Your Side Hustle?

Overview

- A side hustle is meant to accompany your main occupation.

- Side hustles allow greater financial flexibility and the ability to work toward financial goals beyond just paying bills.

- Side hustles come in a wide variety, so it's usually easy to find one that suits your interests and schedule.

Every Friday Was Payday When I Was Growing Up

Back then, there was no such thing as direct deposit, split pay, or payroll cards like we have now, so my dad would bring home a paper check. He would hand it off to my mom, who would use it to take care of the bills. She would give my dad a small allowance out of that money, kind of like George Jetson handing Jane his wallet, and she would take out a few bills to give back to him. So the main job income was used mostly for bills. However, whatever money my dad made on his side hustles, he could keep. With this unspoken rule in mind, my dad had several side hustles. At the top of the list was bootlegging moonshine. For the sake of clarity, please don't see this as me condoning doing anything illegal or dangerous to your health in order to make some extra cash. The possibility of landing in jail and losing your job is too great. It's hard to enjoy a million dollars behind bars.

So, even though I would not encourage you to make yourself a mooning still, or open a bar in your living room, I **will** ask you to be creative. An idea for a side hustle that works with your schedule and uses your talents may not even exist until you think it up.

My dad did actually set up a bar-like atmosphere in our living room on the weekend. It was simple, but lucrative. A handful of local men would come over to the house, have a beer, and let off the steam from a hard week of work. At 5 years old, I would go get the beer out of the fridge as my dad would sell it throughout the day for $1.00 per can. It might not sound like much, but keep in mind that this was the '60s, and even a single dollar had a little more buying power than it does now. Also, he was selling cans for a dollar that he had purchased for thirty-three cents. He would buy a case of twenty-four cans for $8.00. He would spend $8.00 and make $24.00, tripling his initial investment. Genius!

But in order to make that $24.00 per case, several trips back and forth between the refrigerator and the living room would take place. As the official barkeep for each of these evenings, each time I brought a beer back, my dad would always say to me, "Take you a swallow," as a reward. Like many kids growing up, I wanted to be a man in any way that I thought I could. All the respectable adults I knew had jobs, my dad had a job, so I took pride in "working" for my father in his makeshift bar on the weekends. Another thing I saw most of the adults around me do was drink alcohol, so I saw each swig as an act that just took me one step closer to being a "real" man. I would drink as much as I could, just to make my dad proud.

As time went on, my dad decided that he would add gin to the list of items for sale. I didn't have any experience with gin since he had never sold it before. He seemed pretty excited about the idea of adding it to his menu, but I found that a little odd, because gin just looked like plain old water to me. And there was nothing "grown up" about water.

Inevitably, as I was bringing out the half-pints of gin to our paying customers, I was encouraged to drink some. I had felt a little dizzy sometimes after a day of sipping beer, but gin was new territory. It had a strong smell and taste, and it was a dull yellow color. If I could handle beer, I just KNEW I could manage some of the water my dad and his friends called "gin." So, after already having a buzz from beer, mind you, I didn't take just a mere sip of the gin--oh no. I was in pure show off mode. I opened the bottle of gin and drank it down like the tap water I thought it was. When I finished, I remember the entire room letting loose an, "Oooooh!" They were so impressed with me. Their smiles and laughter seemed to me like I was passing some sort of initiation. I could drink with the big boys. I was a real man now!

That night, maybe to also help relieve the pressure of being filled with so much pride, I got a good old stomach pump.

I share this story with you to help you keep in mind that your side hustle should be legal, it does not need to endanger your family, and it does not need to endanger you. At the same time, I want you to understand the spirit of my father's ingenuity. How creative and simple was it to think of selling a cheap product at a decent price in an environment that was comfortable for both him and his clientele?

The earlier chapter titled "Getting to Zero" was all about getting out of debt so that you could take the money that you're earning and use it to its fullest potential. The saying "It takes money to make money" is absolutely true. And until you get out of debt, you're technically not 'making' any money, because it's all being given (or at least is **owed**) to someone else.

Everyone can get a side hustle, and many people already have one.

A side hustle is a way to make some extra cash that allows you flexibility to pursue what you're most interested in. This is often your true passion. For instance, a waitress may work at an auto parts store on her days off from her restaurant, as she works to eventually become a full-time certified mechanic. Or a graphic artist might tutor his classmates for money while he's going through school to get his teaching certification. Side hustles are a great way to delve into your true passion while you hold on to your day job.

It would also be in your best interest to live your passion. Carry business cards around with you, wear a shirt that advertises what you do, or be a walking advertisement for your services. For example, if you're a hairdresser, do your best work on your own head, throw on a shirt with your brand logo on it, or even just a simple "Hair stylist for hire!" Be sure to have business cards handy so that if someone asks, "Who did your hair," you can say, "Me. And I can do yours, too!" Schedule an appointment with them, hand them a card, and enjoy your first sale!

Whether you're at the grocery store, the mall, a party, or the park, always be ready to pitch to someone regarding your services. And if you're still not completely certain what side hustle you should adopt to get yourself some extra money, the next few paragraphs are to help you come up with some ideas to get your creative juices flowing.

Side Hustle Ideas

You are probably hustling already, but you have not monetized it properly. Think of it this way, are you the one that all of your friends call for that particular thing that you do well? Every time a friend gets a new home, do they call you to help decorate? Then you probably have a gift for interior designing. If you are the life of the party and keep everybody laughing all night, then you are likely a good comedian.

It is not about how you make the money, but what you do with it. Do you think a guy who washes cars could make more than an attorney? Yes, he can and, I've seen it done! The key is applying my business principles to whatever you do. A friend of mine who washes cars in Virginia started a car detail business. He details luxury vehicles, and gets to travels to different office complexes. He would detail about 5 cars per day, charging $150 per car. That comes to about $750, plus tips.

However, it is difficult to reach your goal of becoming a millionaire by simply working your side hustle. You must apply Tim's 8 Principles to make your side hustle a financial powerhouse, they are: do it, master it, personalize it, promote it, brand it, monetize it, expand it, and finally, manage it.

1. *Do it.* Do it regularly and consistently. Have you ever seen a new restaurant open up, but they don't keep regular store hours? And the first couple times you went there, the service and food was great, but the next time you go, they aren't open. That probably becomes the last time you will go there.

2. *Master it.* Become the best there is in your industry. If you master something, you become the go-to person. Becoming the master also enables you to charge a premium for your service.

3. *Personalize it.* Offer the client something they can only get from you. If they want that particular item, then they must come to you to get it.

4. *Promote it.* Promoting your idea, or product, is critical. You cannot provide business if nobody knows you're in business.

5. *Brand it.* Distinguish yourself from others. Create a catchphrase, or logo, and be easily accessible.

6. *Monetize it.* This is where you convert your efforts into cash. By promoting, branding, and mastering your industry, you can monetize it at a premium.

7. *Expand it.* Expand on your idea, always improve, and get others to buy into your idea

8. *Manage it.* Carefully manage your efforts. One mistake could be detrimental to your brand. Protect your investment by monitoring it carefully, foreseeing problems, and avoiding them.

Now that you are thinking of your side hustle, consider creating and selling simple products of your own, such as costume jewelry, small home decor (desk organizers, pencil cups, bookends, etc.), or wallets.

Teach a skill. How to change a tire, hand drywall, organize a room, or set up a home Wi-Fi network are all skills that not everyone has, but most people can (and are willing to pay money to) learn. Teach a concept. Do you know everything there is to know about something? Here is a list of general, random ideas to generate extra income to invest. You can take any of these ideas and be successful, but you must be creative with it. However, the best idea is not listed here, because it is in your mind, right now.

- Pet-sit.
- Walk dog.
- Style hair.
- Start a fitness class.
- Do makeup.
- Make clothes.
- Model.
- Print shirts.
- Start a healthy diet cooking class.
- Teach people how to swim.
- Teach people how to shop.
- Be an image consultant.
- Clean houses.
- Clean cars.
- Clean yards.

- Clean parking lots.
- Clean appliances or tools.
- Clean swimming pools.
- Babysit children.
- Care for adults.
- Tutor.
- Teach a language.

Even though these aren't the only ideas to be considered when setting up a side hustle, these are helpful to take into account when you are thinking about coming up with your own. The major things to look out for when considering a side hustle are:

- It's something you enjoy (or at least can tolerate for an extended period of time).
- It's something that comes naturally to you, so it doesn't feel like a lot of extra work.
- It's something that's tied to what your dream job would be, so that the experience will help you out in the future when you're running your own business in that industry.
- It's something that doesn't cost you a lot of money, time, energy, or safety to do.

As long as your side hustle meets this criteria, then you will likely make a lot of money outside of your day job, and you'll probably enjoy doing it at the same time. A win-win situation!

The previous chapter "Getting to 0" was primarily about getting out of debt, and allowing the money you are currently earning to make its full potential. However, it is very important to increase the income that you are making because you have to have money to invest, and the old saying is true, "It takes money to make money." Everyone has a side hustle, and they all are unique. Be creative and do not be afraid to offer something or do something that is not currently being done! The key is to identify the need or to recognize a problem and offer a creative (out of the box solution).

Work That Hustle

When I was living in Virginia, I was going through my second divorce (the one I mentioned in my introduction). I was losing the fight against my ex-wife big time. It felt like her dream team of attorneys were always three steps ahead of me. It felt like even MY lawyer was working for her!

On the very last day (thank goodness!) of the court proceedings, I said to the judge, "You can take my house, my money, and my possession, but you can't take my f-ing hustle." However true that statement was then, and is now, that probably wasn't the most appropriate setting to let it be known. But, even in the midst of all that turmoil and chaos, I believed that your greatest assets were things that no one could take from you, no matter how hard they try: your time and your drive. I was eager for the legal process to end so I could reinvent myself at a new starting line. I understood that time was precious, and every day I spent not working on my map was one more day of my life that I would spend without my million in hand. My hustle was critical and could not be copied, destroyed, or limited, and could not be taken from me. This is what I want to instill in **you** as someone hustling toward their first million. You can never hustle too hard. There is always room to hustle more. The harder you hustle, the faster you will arrive at your destination--your millionaire status.

Your desire to become a millionaire will not just happen by mistake. Yes, good things MAY come to those who wait, but only the things left by those who hustle. Don't wait another day for the things that you deserve and desire. If you get out and hustle, then you can have what you may have tomorrow, today. I'd rather hustle 24/7 than be a slave from 9 to 5.

So much of your creativity, time, and energy is lost when you work a standard 9 to 5. We've all done it at some point. But this book is about using a 9 to 5 as a jumping off point toward bigger and better things. How badly do you want to get away from alarm clocks forcing you awake when your body is exhausted and requires more rest? Aren't you tired of having ideas that will make your workplace run more smoothly, or most cost-efficiently, only to be ignored? No more having to come in when the boss wants you to, and no more having to stretch a dollar until the next paycheck. No more being paid the same amount of money week after week, and month after month, even when the company you work for is making millions or billions in profits every single quarter. No more hoping and praying that your good work will be noticed, and you'll eventually get a promotion that will definitely come with more responsibility, but may or may not come with a comparable pay raise. No more limits on life, you only have one, live it to the fullest!

When you work for yourself, build your own wealth, and call your own shots, you can express yourself freely, live a life that you choose, engage in business on your terms, and always make what you're worth. Not the bare minimum that it is legal to be given.

Anything will work if you hustle hard enough to make it work. One thing I always say to people when they run their hustle idea past me is, "Anything will work if you work it, or hustle hard enough for it." I especially say that when I really can't see the person's vision they are conveying. Not everyone can see what you see. Your hustle will be something that you can get value out of, while other people cannot, or are unwilling to.

I was talking to the funeral home director in my hometown about real-estate, and we were talking finance and investing. He asked me about getting into the housing business. He stated that it appeared difficult to him, and he wasn't sure if he could do it. I told him that the key thing about real estate is being able to recognize value, and extracting that value. I have become good at recognizing value. Likewise, if I see a dead body, I am a little taken back, but he has the ability to recognize and extract the value from that dead body.

Keep Your Side Hustle Legal

The phrase "crime doesn't pay" is not just a slogan, it is the truth! There is more misfortune than profit gained from committing a crime. When I speak to young people who are considered "at risk," and think criminal activity is a quick and easy way to become wealthy, I ask them how many drug dealers they know who are retired and receiving passive income from their drug dealing. I pause for a minute and wait for a response. I often say, "If you did know one, then let me know, and I will turn them in to the authorities." Society and social media has done an excellent job of lying to our youth and old people alike. They claim there are no consequences to crime.

I had been working in my church for years, and one of my duties was to accompany my Pastor to the jails to assist and counsel people who are facing serious charges. I sat with countless families and saw them mortgage their homes and sell their possessions to hire an attorney to keep their loved ones from going to prison for a long period of time, or life. Sometimes successful and sometimes not, but one thing was consistent, it was very expensive. So let me be the first to correct the phrase "crime doesn't pay," to "crime doesn't pay the criminal, it pays the police and attorneys."

Make sure your side hustle makes sense. There's nothing worse than a dumb side hustle. Dumb side hustles are simply hustling backwards. Hustling backwards is when you spend more time, effort, and energy working, rather than receiving benefits. If that is your situation, then you do not have a hustle, you have a hobby.

Don't ever let anyone tell you "no!" This is very important to conceptualize. Just FYI, if you are a person that will take no for an answer easily, you will not succeed. There is no such thing as a definitive "No," because there is always another route to take. Many times you are closer than you think to obtaining a "Yes." I truly believe no person has the inherent right to tell someone else "No" in reference to attaining your goals. In this journey to your million, "No" is not an option! You have access to everything that you need to make your million, and you just have to recognize it and tap into it! "No" is negative, and is designed to disallow and stop progress, therefore a no is useless to you.

Always go the extra mile in conducting fair and reasonable business practices. I have been in the real-estate business for nearly 30 years now at some capacity, as a buyer, real-estate agent, builder, and flipper. I have done business with a lot of different characters. One thing that I have found remain constant is, if you do honest work at a fair rate, then those are the successful business people with thriving businesses. On the contrary, you have individuals conducting businesses that have low moral standards, and will scam you in a hot second. Please remember that you lose much more than you gain when you conduct business in an unscrupulous manner.

On a recent house flip project, I was getting my estimates from general contractors. The contractor who provided the lowest bid, gave a significantly lower bid than the other 2 estimates I received, and he guaranteed the work would be done in a fast, professional manner. The bid was low enough for me to take the risk, and I knew he had low-balled the price to attain follow on work, which I was OK with. Also, I understood that any unseen issues would be renegotiated for the contractor to make a profit. Well, I make mistakes also, I paid too much too fast in the draw schedule, and when he got most of his money, he was nowhere to be found. Yes, shame on me! Well, unfortunately for him, he didn't realize how persistent I was, and he thought I would simply cut my losses and walk away. I didn't do that, but that's what I recommend that you do if in this situation. He blocked my phone number, and every number I called him from. In this area, at the local Home Depots and Lowe's, customers get contractor information and call them from the stores. That's how contractors get much of their business. Well, he blocked all the numbers I called him from, so I just called him from every Home Depot and Lowe's in the local area. I had a little birdie inform me that he didn't know why his business dropped so significantly over the past several months, and he finally unblocked my number, and by doing so, he unblocked Lowe's and Home Depot. He apologized and asked if I had any additional work for him. I accepted his apology and told him that I believed his business would pick up again.

You benefit heavily in the long-term from being fair and honest. Now, see what happens when you do right by people. In every situation, do your best to correct the misunderstanding. I know that some people are impossible to please, but still do your very best. Maintaining a fair workplace is always top priority when building a business. If you're thinking about becoming your own boss, be sure to keep this in mind: You might be saying to yourself, "Now, Tim, you're talking all this millionaire stuff, but I ain't got no job!" Well, no job, no problem, hire yourself. You need zero degrees, zero certificates, zero recommendations, and zero resumes to be the owner/CEO of your own company. Even if you are currently employed by a stable job, you can still work for yourself and promote your business. Companies today are not as loyal as they were in the past, therefore you owe it to yourself to be prepared. One of my favorite recommendations to someone unemployed: I ask them what was the last job that they applied for? The next question is: What does the company do? With a follow-up question: Do you think you are the best person for the job? Do you see where I am going with this? If you have the same knowledge this employer does, and you are great at it, then start a rival company and out-perform them so they regret not hiring you!

Chapter 5: How Money Works

"Wisdom is a shelter as money is a shelter, but the advantage of knowledge is this: Wisdom preserves those who have it." --Ecclesiastes 7:12

Overview

- It's difficult to manage anything that you don't understand---and that includes money.
- Remember this Doppio Lesson: Lump sums aren't always the best option.
- Being patient with money is a big part of managing it well.

93

- With income, as with most things in life, it's helpful to avoid putting all your eggs in one basket.
- There are about as many ways to make money as there are ways to invest it.
- Any time someone tells you that their investment can make you a millionaire overnight, be careful!

I became "The Millionaire Maker" at a toast during a Navy retirement ceremony. I had a small speaking role, and before I went up to speak, the retiree announced, "Listening to Tim's advice and following his guidance, my wife and I are able to retire much earlier than we ever thought imaginable, so toast to Tim, The Millionaire Maker." To be completely transparent, this was three weeks after I couldn't buy gas to get home on payday. I was a little angry. Then the epiphany came to me. If they became millionaires listening to my advice, then I will listen to my own advice and become a millionaire also. So, let me tell you some of the principals I shared with them on how money works.

Numbers don't lie, people do. Unfortunately, that is a very true statement that is proven often. Nothing is as good or bad as it appears when it comes to finances, as well as life. Numbers are predictable, because 1 plus 1 will always equal 2, therefore once you understand how money works and you learn the predictability of numbers, it will be exciting to get to the point of drawing your map to your million. Everyone wants to make more money, however, very few people truly understand how money works. That is not a knock on anyone's intelligence, because there is so much misleading information out there. Getting a proper understanding of how money works is the only way to develop your map to your million.

Many times when I meet with clients, I run a little financial literacy quiz on them, one of the oldest tricks in the book, the old compound interest penny chart. I was always amazed how many people got this wrong. One technique I used was, I scavenged up as many pennies as I could muster within the occupants of the room. I was careful to remember how many pennies each individual gave me, so I could return them to their rightful owners. I informed them that their pennies would be returned, but one penny may be altered when it was returned. This usually sparked enough attention for the penny lenders to listen to the lesson that I gave. I took one penny, held it in the air, and shook it as if I just placed a magic spell on it. I chanted, "Doppio, doppio, doppio," which means double in Italian, but this had absolutely no significance, I just liked the way that "doppio" sounded, and it got the crowd going. Then, I took that penny and I placed it on the table before the trainee, and gave them a choice. They could take this doppio penny, and whoever was the holder of the doppio penny would have the power to double his or her money for 31 consecutive days. However, if they accepted this doppio penny, then that was the only starting amount of money they could accept: one penny. Or, they could have a one time payment of $100,000.00 with no special powers to add to all the wealth they had already attained.

I usually got the, "Give me my 100K" response, and I played along and said, "Wait, before you make a final decision," I then started adding pennies to the table and said, "Don't forget that tomorrow you can have 2 pennies," and then I kept the show going until I got to day 5, and I had 16 cents on the table. Then, I asked for a final decision, and I still got, "Give me my 100K." I said, "Sure, but let's take a look at compound interest." By day 21, the doppio penny was now worth $10,485.76. Here was where it got interesting. By day 31, the doppio penny was now worth $10,737,418.24, which was over 10 times the, "Give me my 100K" blunder.

Once the show was over, all of the pennies were mixed up on the table, and I started the return process. I made an announcement that one of these pennies was an actual doppio penny, and all of a sudden the careless attitudes of those pennies suddenly went away.

Day	Amount
1	$0.01
2	$0.02
3	$0.04
4	$0.08
5	$0.16
6	$0.32
7	$0.64
8	$1.28
9	$2.56
10	$5.12
11	$10.24
12	$20.48
13	$40.96
14	$81.92
15	$163.84
16	$327.68
17	$655.36
18	$1,310.72
19	$2,621.44
20	$5,242.88
21	$10,485.76
22	$20,971.52
23	$41,943.04
24	$83,886.08
25	$167,772.16
26	$335,544.32
27	$671,088.64
28	$1,342,177.28
29	$2,684,354.56
30	$5,368,709.12
31	$10,737,418.24

It is important to have "rules of thumb" tools in your financial toolbox. The English phrase rule of thumb refers to "A means of estimation made according to a rough and ready practical rule, not based on science or exact measurement" *(Phrases.org.uk)*. Basically, a rule of thumb is a quick formula in your head to get you in the financial ballpark. I am sure you will remember the doppio penny exercise as a rule of thumb, but one of my favorites is the "Rule of 72." The "Rule of 72" is a simplified way to determine how long an investment will take to double, given a fixed annual rate of interest. By dividing 72 by the annual rate of return, investors can receive a rough estimate of how many years it will take for the initial investment to duplicate itself. For example, if you are offered a 20% interest return on investment ROI, dividing 20 into 72 is 3.6, therefore it would take 3.6 years for your money to double. In other words, if you invest 50K at 20%, you will have 100K in 3.6 years, 200K in 7.2 years, and 400K in a little over ten years. It is important to realize these facts. Most people say, "I ain't got 50K just laying around the house to invest," and I then see them drive off in a 70K Mercedes Benz that is depreciating in value as fast as they can make their $1,000.00+ monthly payment. Which would you rather have in 10 years: a 10 year old Benz with high mileage, or \$400,000.00? You make the choice, but now you know the truth of what that luxury item is costing you.

The Millionaire Maker Designates Three Financial Phases of Life: Learning Years, Earning Years, Rewarding Years

These three phases all have distinct purposes. There is no exact age you need to be for each of the phases, because of varying life paths and circumstances. However, the general learning years are from birth to approximately twenty-four years old. Earning years tend to run from about twenty-five to fifty-five, and then finally your rewarding years. It is important to recognize these phases when building wealth, because they help you recognize how narrow these windows are. You must take full advantage of them, because time is of the essence. In all the financial phases, you will be learning, earning, and rewarding yourself, but recognizing what phase you are in, and where you are in that phase, should indicate how time much you partake in each. For example, in your learning phase, you go to school year round and learn 10 months out of the year. You work a summer job for 1.5 months, with two weeks off on Spring Break and summer vacation rewarding yourself for a good year. On the contrary, a person in their rewarding years should be vacationing 10 months of the year rewarding themselves, 1.5 months of consulting younger generations, and a couple of weeks in a course, or exploring new things. Now do you see the difference?

One of the main points to take away from this section is: Don't be discouraged, no matter where you fall in the three phases with your current situation. The key is to recognize and respond. Remember, your map to your million can take as little as seven years from absolute zero. The ultimate goal is to learn as much as you can in the learning years. Earn as much as you can in your earning years. Reward yourself as much as you can in your rewarding years. Let me give you a brief description of some general things that you should be focusing on during each phase of your financial life.

Learning years - Roughly from age 1-24. You must be exploring as many career paths as possible. You can't learn as much as possible if you don't know what to study. Reading books and utilizing the internet gives you an advantage over previous generations that were limited. Broaden your horizons by looking at careers outside your community, culture, country, or race. Remember to explore other cultures. Shut off past generations biases, this could limit you by poisoning your perception of something that could be your passion. For example, if your dad and granddad were in the Air Force, but you preferred the Navy, and they hated the

Navy, don't be easily persuaded. Identify your richest aunt, uncle, or other family member, and make yourself their new favorite. Not to try and be included in the will (that wouldn't hurt, though), but obviously they did something right, and it wouldn't hurt for them to be one of your mentors. Finally, protect yourself and guard your future. In your youth, you are faced with many distractions, and one mistake could limit your earning years dramatically, because you are at the beginning stage. Stay out of trouble!

Earning years - Roughly from age 25-55. You must be earning as much as possible, because after age 55, your earning potential goes down dramatically. Your desire to work decreases, and the perception of you being outdated increases. I am not saying this is right, but I am saying this is how it is. You should limit your rewarding years to a reasonable amount, due to the fact your ultimate goal should be getting your rewarding years as soon as possible. If you read this book at age 25 and execute the principals, then you can reach your rewarding years by age 32. Whatever age you are, draw your map to your million as early as possible. It is more important to make good strategic moves with your money now, than to make a great deal of money and not have any in your later years.

Rewarding years - Beginning around age 56. You must do what you want to do. The hardest thing is shifting your mindset and habits late in life. Reward yourself as much as you can, and protect your wealth, because the individuals who didn't read my book are looking around for those with money, and they are ready to hookup.

Diversification

One of the earliest mistakes that new investors make is the lack of diversification. That is largely because new investors are trying to build, and they desire seeing bigger numbers, or larger deals, instead of spreading the investment and reducing risks. That is a common and understandable mistake, and that is why I set aside a total section to stress the importance of diversification.

"Diversification is the act or practice of manufacturing a variety of products, investing in a variety of securities, selling a variety of merchandise, etc., so that a failure in or an economic slump affecting one of them will not be disastrous" (Dictionary.com).

Diversification maximizes returns by investing in dissimilar, or diverse areas that would each respond in a different way to the exact same world event. For example, if there were a crisis in the housing market, then it would have different effects on the automobile market than the retail market. Most investment professionals agree that diversification is the most important factor when reaching and sustaining long-range financial goals while minimizing risk. However, it does not guarantee the investor will never take a loss.

The rewards of diversification are to reduce risk, and naturally provide multiple small streams of income, which is better than one big river of income. This is because if one of several small streams become contaminated, then it does not affect the other streams, therefore causing you less disruption.

How to diversify: Pick things to invest in that are dissimilar, and you have a good understanding in. Avoid linear investments. For example, don't invest in cows and milk, because if the cow market goes, then the milk market will also be affected. Another common mistake is investing on competing markets. Some financial experts thinks this is a great idea, however to me, it is similar to the Dallas Cowboys playing the Washington Redskins in the Super Bowl. If you bet 10 dollars on each team, then you are really not gaining anything. Diversification is tricky, and just like market surveillance, you should always be looking for ways to diversify.

When is Diversification Not a Good Thing?

When you are too diversified and you lose your span of control. You must maintain adequate surveillance over all of your investments, which is why you should limit your diversification. Also, when you diversify into areas where you have minimum knowledge, that could place you in a vulnerable position. You would not recognize market warning signs and turbulence. This also places you at risk of being taken advantage of from other more seasoned experts in that particular area. All is fair in love, war, and business. Therefore, *caveat emptor,* which is a Latin term that means "Let the buyer beware," is similar to the phrase "Sold as is." This term means that the buyer assumes the risk that a product may fail to meet expectations, or it may have defects.

The Importance of Passive Income

Passive income is critical to your success in your map to your million. The number one way to secure passive income is ownership!

There are not enough hours in the day to work an hourly wage, and earn enough for you to truly live a healthy and rewarding life. There must be a healthy balance between work and life. Let me explain what I mean, in any given 24-hour workday, you are not just giving your employer 8 hours, you are giving them a lot more of your life. Of that 24 hours, you have to get dressed for work, travel to work, and then work possibly 9 hours. Then, you travel home from work in rush hour traffic, get undressed, and then prepare for the next workday. That is extremely time consuming for 9 hours of pay, and that is only an example of the average employee. Without investing, you have created yourself one single point of financial failure.

As you reduce your work obligation, you need to increase your passive income. I call this making money even when you are sleeping.

Years ago, a popular, but dangerous, party spot was ran by an associate of mine. This club was always going through its ups and downs, however it stayed open for several years. Even through bar fights, shootings, and sexual assault accusations. Finally, as the area gentrified and became more family-oriented, the club was forced to close. My associate approached me to inquire about assistance in finding another location. I surveyed the area and gave him a number of possibilities for him to consider purchasing. He quickly returned to me and asked for a rental list, not a purchase list, because he had been renting the club for that time. Between economic hard times and high rent costs, he was unable to save any significant cash. I was shocked, because I thought he was the owner that whole time. In fact, he only physically saw the true owner a few times over the course of several years of paying rent to him. The owner was making money in his sleep, while my associate worked the long hours, and accepted the related risk of operating a club type business. My associate felt my frustration and he stated, "I had to feed my family." I respected that, but I responded, "No, you took care of his family."

Two Buckets and Two Sticks

There is value and money in everything under the sun. You just need to have the ability to recognize that value, and extract it. What do I mean there is value in everything? Give me a list of ten random things, and I will give you an example of how it is valuable, and also often times accessible to everyone. There is value in talking. Most everyone can speak, yet people get paid for speeches every day. There is value in words. People write blogs and articles. There's value in hot days, just ask the HVAC technician. There is value in punching, see Mike Tyson. There is value in dead bodies, just ask the undertaker. The point is, you can't name anything that does not have an associated value. However, you must have the vision to recognize that value, coupled with the ability and determination to extract and monetize that value. It frustrates me when I meet people with limited opportunity attitudes.

A new hotel was being constructed on the beach one summer. An unemployed construction worker was frustrated by not being able to land employment on the project. Falling on real hard times, he became homeless on the beach and hoped for opportunity to present itself. Walking the beach one afternoon, I ran into the construction worker, and I recognized him from a previous project he worked on. He shared with me his story and expressed his frustrations of not being able to earn any money. I really felt bad for him as we stood there within view of the hotel construction site.

I pointed to the construction site, and excitedly asked, "Do you see what I see?" He looked diligently and stated, "No, I can't see it." I stated to him again, "Look closer!" The truth is, I actually didn't see anything either, but I was attempting to make him see an opportunity that was previously overlooked. Suddenly, he yelled, "I see it! I see it!" He ran towards the construction site and approached the overflowing dumpster. He dived in and came out with two buckets and two sticks. I said to myself with disappointment, "Oh well, you can't help everybody," and walked away.

A few hours later, I was ready to head home. I was on my way to my car when I heard a nice beat and a crowd of people dancing. I wanted to see what was going on, so pushed through the crowd to the center. There he was with his two buckets and two sticks playing the drums, and getting tipped very well. He made more money that night than he would have made in a week on the construction site. So, the next time that you feel that you have limited, or no opportunity, look. Look closer.

Rental Property Do's and Don'ts

Rental property is a great wealth builder and can provide excellent passive income. I recommend real-estate being a major portion of getting your million. Here are some of the tips and lessons I learned over the years, the hard way, and I'll let you learn it the easy way. So, I'm going to list some rental property dos and don'ts for you to follow that will save you a lot of time, hassle, and money. I get asked about real-estate often, and how to get in the business. The first piece of advice I give is to "stack your cash," because real-estate is an expensive game to play, and you must have your finances in order. I see many people getting loans to purchase rental properties. Let's say their payment to the mortgage company is $800.00 per month, and they are charging in rent $1,200.00. Wow, that is $400.00 a month profit, that's great, right? No, that is not! Ok, let's look at the real world. Factor in annual taxes, insurance, repairs, and administration, your return on investment is minimal. This scenario is only acceptable when you have a property that is rapidly appreciating in value, and you are managing it closely. Stacking your cash allows you to purchase a less expensive property cash, and that allows you a higher ROI, and a much safer investment, because you do not have the finance charges. In the scenario mentioned, what if the tenant loses a job and can't pay rent for a couple of months? That scenario becomes a nightmare.

Some things can fall in the do and don't categories, like conducting a credit check, I know what you are thinking, "Don't do a credit check?!" A credit check can be misleading, so my little work around is, I tell the applicant that no matter how bad their credit is, if they list the event on the application, and provide an explanation, then I will not count that against them. This usually works, and I get a pretty more accurate picture of their situation, and also how they think. You must realize that you are entering into a business relationship with this individual for at least a year. I don't discriminate against people with bad credit. I sometimes even welcome a person with some credit issues, because even though I provide very nice homes, you want to cut your turnover as much as possible. A tenant with credit issues has limited options, and are not so quick to move to the new subdivision down the street. Another thing that I may or may not do is call references, especially the "previous landlord." The references they provide are their best friend, boyfriend, girlfriend, sister, brother, and the "previous landlord" is usually their mother! You can quickly tell when the "previous landlord" is their mom or boyfriend, because they go overboard on their recommendation. I got one recommendation so good that at the end of the phone call the "previous landlord" asked, "Will the applicant get the place?" I replied, "With the description you just provided, I think I will have them move in with me!"

Another unique thing I may or may not do is take an application fee. I remember my niece was looking for an apartment, and she was charged application fees just to get turned down, and that made me upset. A person is going through enough looking for a new place. An old scam is when a person lists a home on *Craigslist*, and it sounds perfect. There are no credit or background checks, and the only catch is you must come today between these strict time frames, and pay a small $100.00 application fee. This guy is setting up ten applicants a day, and not in any rush to lease the place.

He's making more money on application fees than if the property were rented. Don't do this, karma is very real. I only take an application if I am seriously considering that applicant, to ensure they are serious, and to cover my time. Another trick of the trade is, before you sign a lease with them, take a trip to their current residence. Call them when you are "near their neighborhood," even though you actually just performed a satisfactory drive-by inspection of the exterior of their property. They forgot to "sign" a page, and you just need a quick signature. You stop in and get the signature, but wait, all of a sudden you have to use the bathroom. That trip to and from the bathroom will tell you everything that you need to know.

Do:

1. Have your finances together first.

2. Provide nice homes.

3. Renovate with better quality materials.

4. Drive-bys.

5. Make repairs quickly.

6. Maintain good insurance.

7. Communicate with tenants.

8. Develop a clear lease.

9. Select long term tenants.

10. Be available to your tenants.

Don't:

1. Discriminate.

2. Keep utilities in your name.

3. Allow late and partial payment.

4. Raise rent too much for long term tenant.

5. Go paperless.

6. Neglect minor repairs.

7. Allow illegal activity.

8. Be a slumlord.

9. Throw away receipts.

Chapter 6: A New Way of Thinking

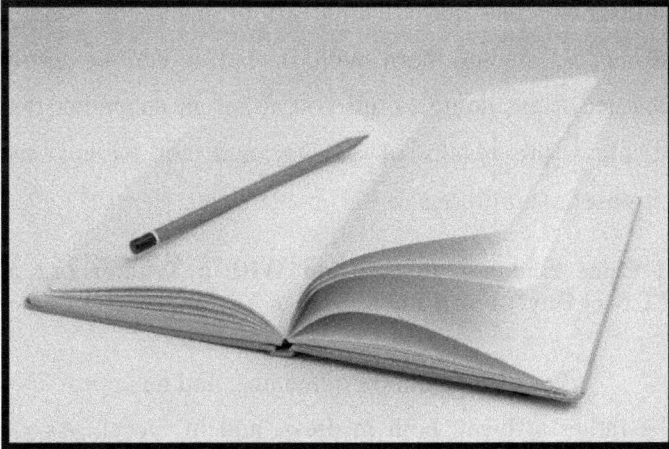

Overview

- With income, as with most things in life, it's helpful to avoid putting all your eggs in one basket.
- There are about as many ways to make money as there are ways to invest it.
- Any time someone tells you that their investment can make you a millionaire overnight, be careful!

The mind of a millionaire does not mean he is always counting money, or the CEO of a large company making million dollar deals every day. The mind of a millionaire has mastered the art of managing wealth. Some people are born with it, but it can be easily learned. I am going to tell you about an encounter that displays the results of having, and not having, the mindset of a millionaire.

I Once Had a Conversation With a Trainer (a.k.a. 'Towel Boy') For a Local Sports Team

We were about the same age, and he appeared to be rather affluent, both in dress, and in speech. As we smoked our way too expensive cigars (sorry, you can't be thrifty on everything) in the team's lounge one day, he shared with me his path to financial freedom. He said that, as a professional sports trainer, he was always around large amounts of money, and a whole lot of futility. He saw many young athletes get a major sports contract, only to find that it was too much money too soon. More often than not, these young men made at least one, but usually a series, of ill-advised financial decisions.

Even though I don't think it's very kind to take pleasure in someone else's downfall, Towel Boy seemed proud to share the endless stories of situations in which he had more wealth than most of the professional sports players he was working under. Towel Boy lived below his means, he was persistent, and he could be very cunning. He took pride in rattling the names of individuals that he knew had large windfalls of money at one time, but who were now completely broke. I could see a gleam in his eye when he pointed out one of his two Bentley's that he owns--both of which were purchased from players when they got themselves into financial trouble. I do, however, give Towel Boy credit for his hard work, strong work ethic, and being savvy enough to take advantage of a situation that could benefit him financially. However, I thought he was the type of man that should be a lesson for everyone who finds themselves with a large amount of funds readily available. Someone like Towel Boy is always lurking around people with a lot of money, and trying to trick them out of every dime. Or, just waiting to swoop in at a low moment and take advantage of someone, instead of helping them.

I got up and left the cigar lounge. Towel Boy called out, "Tim, where you going, bro? Let's get together later and discuss business!" Don't get me wrong, I love capitalism, but I believe in doing right by others, because I believe karma is real. So I just responded, "I don't have a Bentley for you, Towel Boy!"

If you want a millionaire status, then start thinking like one! You can't conceive what you cannot conceptualize. Remember that all millionaires are not permanent millionaires, because some individuals could have made a great deal of money in a short period of time, without having a millionaire mindset. Once I heard the greatest saying, "A fool and his money are soon separated." You see this almost every day with entertainers and sports figures. They are soon broke after their short careers, and their managers and handlers are wealthy at a relatively young age. Becoming wealthy can be easy, if you consider how some of the entertainers and sports figures obtain their wealth, sometimes easy come, easy go.

My Recommended Characteristics of a Millionaire--Don't be a Towel Boy

- Focused on specific goals.
  - It is difficult to stay focused long-term on one thing in today's multitasking society, but finances take patience and persistence.
  - Don't get so many ideas that it paralyzes your movement on a smaller set of goals.

- Able to link goals and events together.

- Doing things that has no lasting value is only wasting time, and time is the most valuable asset that you have. Be able to recognize a good return on investment.
- Everything you do should play a small part of your overall goal, and your map to your million.
- With every endeavor you enter, you should ask yourself, "How is this going to help me for the rest of my life?"

- Good negotiator.
  - A millionaire is a good and fair negotiator.
  - Always look for the "win-win" scenario.
  - Never negotiate like this is the last deal in the world.
  - Never take advantage of someone because of their situation.

- Avoid spendthrift friends.
  - Always screen the company you keep. Don't be the guy who picks up the tab every time.
  - Avoid relationships (boyfriend/girlfriend/ wife) with financially troubled individuals. A financially sound individual should feel as if they can bring the financially challenged individual up, but it is usually the opposite.

- An expert at goal setting.
  - Your map to your million is highly dependent on accurate goal setting. The better you are at goal setting, the easier your journey to millionaire status will be.
  - Avoid setting too lofty goals, because it will make you immune to success.
  - Avoid setting too minor goals, because it slows progress.
  - A good goal should excite you and scare you at the same time.

- Avoid debt.
  - Not all debt is bad, but debt should be avoided, if possible.
  - Debt is an interference to wealth building.

- Know financial position at all times.
  - To make good financial decisions, you must know your true financial position. Many people purchase so many houses, cars, and consumables that they cannot afford, because they are unaware of their true financial reality.
  - You don't know which way to go if you don't know where you are.

- Know how money works.
  - You should study the concepts in this book, and use this book as a reference.
  - Have rules of thumb, as we covered in earlier chapters, like the Rule of 72, and double a penny a day for 31 days.

- Create multiple sources of income.
  - Diversification gives an investor added security.
  - Your job can be your trap, if you become too dependent on it.
  - Constantly seek diversification opportunities, but avoid overextending yourself and getting into investments that you have minimum knowledge in.
  - The more sources of income that you establish, the less dependent you become on one single source. This is a key principle.

- Seek wise counsel.
  - Never think you know it all.
  - Always speak with other financial experts, use what they know, and add your own unique approach.
  - The blind cannot lead the blind.

- Shop at GW Fashion.
  - This is my favorite. "GW Fashion" is my code name for Goodwill, I love thrifting!
  - This is an example of living below your means, and also a side hustle opportunity. Over the past several years, I have purchased several items from "GW Fashion" that was worth many times what I paid.
  - The poorest people I know are too proud to shop at Goodwill. Don't be that way.

- Make money in your sleep.
  - Passive income is key, you want to get away from trading time on the clock for money, there are not enough hours in the day.

- Speak with authority.
  - A millionaire knows their financial strength.
  - A millionaire knows what he or she can do.

- Inspire others.
  - Your family and friends watch your moves closer than you think.
  - Your financial strength will determine generations to come behind you.

A New Way of Thinking About Money: The Power of Two Minds on Wealth Building

The power of two is greater than the sum of both. Let me explain, having two individuals work together gives a great advantage financially. My favorite recommendation for couples that desire to be millionaires, is to live off one salary, and invest the other for 3 years. After that statement, I pause for a while and let the couple roll their eyes. I usually get the response, "We can't afford that, we have kids and BMWs," or any other excuse under the sun. I wait until I hear all the excuses they have to offer, and then I calmly state with conviction, "You can't afford *not* to." I give them this scenario: What if one of you loses your job? You will live off of one salary, but will not have the luxury of banking the other. You can make a living off of one salary fun, like a game, when you are doing it by choice and seeing the increase. It's not much fun when the situation is forced upon you, and you are experiencing the decrease. Jobs in this society are not like the days of old, where you stay employed for 30 consecutive years, and they give you a gold watch, and a retirement check at the end. In current society, employers and employees are less loyal to each other, and more concerned with immediate company profits. Therefore, think of this as a drill for the inevitable, and when the actual event does occur, you are prepared and know the steps that you need to take.

The power of two doesn't have to be a husband and wife combination, it can be any relationship combination. When it is a joint venture of an alternative situation, clear requirements and expectations must be established in the beginning. Also, don't dive directly in. Give yourself a short trial period in the beginning where either, or both, of you can simply walk away from the arrangement. However, give it a good try, because the reward is potentially great. Set clear goals and monitor them closely. Be careful not to let yourself slip into a worse situation by developing bad spending habits. You actually can walk away from this situation in a worse position than when you started.

The Power of Having Money and Wealth vs. The Power of Not Having Money and Wealth

People without money or wealth are the most taken advantage of around the world, even here in the United States. Most often, people who need it most, and have the least, are charged a higher rate, and sometimes higher prices. They are charged more for the same items, due to risk, and not given the "bulk discount" by using the economy of scale. In poor neighborhoods, even gas is more expensive than in other areas.

My Pastor, Dr. Jake Manley, would always preach financial security. He would always say to the congregation, "If they were selling brand new Cadillac's in the parking lot for $1,000.00 a piece, for everyone who had $1,000.00 cash, some of you wouldn't be able to buy one." That statement would get people to assess their personal situation. It was never meant to embarrass anyone, only to inspire.

If you don't work now to put yourself in a financial situation where you can take advantage of a $1,000.00 brand new Cadillac, then you will only stand by and watch others get their brand new Cadillac in front of your helpless eyes. People in bad financial situations are often used to secure the financial future of others. Here is an actual true and sad story that I personally witnessed in Atlanta, Georgia. An investor purchased a distressed property, in the hood, near the Georgia Dome. The investor only paid $13,000.00 for the home, and didn't want to invest much more money in the home. The investor rented the home to a handyman for a reduced rent amount of $675.00 per month, as long as he makes improvements within the home as time goes by. The area was extremely neglected by the residents in the community. The handyman dealt with crime, poor conditions, drugs, and neglect for over a decade, for the low price of $675.00 per month. The investor didn't make many improvements, because he knew that the handyman had few to no other options for residence.

Now, fast forward 10 years. The new Mercedes Benz stadium is complete, and business is booming around the city. The home that was purchased for $13,000.00, is now worth $175,000.00. Guess what, the investor kicked out the handyman and his family. I think that is as wrong as two left shoes. The handyman and his family become poorer, and the investor becomes wealthier. Don't get me wrong, I don't blame the investor, I would have done the exact same thing. I blame the handyman for not taking advantage of the numerous "$1,000.00 brand new Cadillac" situations that were available to him over the past decade. Don't be that person, read this book carefully, follow the key principles, increase your financial power, and live a more abundant life for you and your loved ones. Be alert and have the mind of the investor.

Hood Rich

If you are on any kind of public assistance, get off. Think about it for a second, who is really the benefactor for public assistance? In economically challenged neighborhoods, there are very few businesses that actually conduct business in those areas. Sometimes the areas are labeled as "food deserts," meaning an urban area in which it is difficult to buy affordable, or good-quality fresh food. Many Americans live in food deserts where they have corner stores with chips, sodas, and don't forget beer, there is plenty of "food," but none of it healthy. In those areas, like all over America, some of the residents receive food stamps. I understand that food stamps are not a bad thing, and are needed by some. However, the real benefactor for the food stamp program is the corner store that is in the middle of that area selling poor quality at a super high price. It is free money. The food stamp recipient is simply the method of making the corner store owner, and their families wealthy. Much in the same with housing, the residents who live in the substandard subsidized housing is only the means for getting the subsidy payment in the investor/owners account. Often times, public assistance is an economic trap that forces families to grow dependent on them, and simply passing that dependency on to the next generation. So, think about it, you will never achieve wealth on public assistance. Therefore, if you are on any kind of public assistance, get off!

Two Car Payments Trap

New cars are one of the worst investments that you can ever make, and the more you spend on automobiles, the less likely you will reach your financial

127

goals. New car purchases have such a diminishing return. Once you sign on the dotted line to drive away with your brand new car, no matter how good of a "deal" you got on it, the car value drops up to 20% the first 100 feet that you drive it off the lot. No matter how you slice it, losing 20% in value from an investment immediately is a seriously bad investment. Next time you purchase a brand new car, I want you to try this, immediately after you sign the papers and get your keys, I want you to turn to the salesperson and try to sell the car back to them. "I want to sell the car back to you, how much can I get?" You will be shocked by the offer you get back. An average new car drops 20% (add to top) in value by the time you sign the papers. Try this before you even sit in the car, and you will see that they don't want it back. They just sold you something that they are not willing to buy. You should feel real frustrated by then. In today's society, so much emphasis is placed on what we drive, it has become more of a projection of wealth and power, than just a means of transportation. I now look at the people who are driving those $80,000.00-$100,000.00 cars and that doesn't tell me that they are wealthy or powerful, but it definitely informs me that they have $80,000.00-$100,000.00 poorly invested in a diminishing return. To make things even worse, car prices have gone through the roof! There was a time not long ago when only the foreign luxury cars were over $50,000.00. However, now even some mid size American cars can top $50,000.00. When I counsel with people, nothing is more frustrating than seeing individuals sink more into their luxury sedans and trucks than they have in savings, and 401K combined. Also, here is another tip - Never ever have more than one car payment. Even if you are a dual income family, stay away from the 2 car payment trap. The 2 car payment trap has a way of just stretching the family budget a little too far. I understand the need to have and maintain reliable transportation, however reliable transportation does not have to be too expensive. Today, gently used or off lease cars are very reliable, and much less expensive to purchase. Now with Uber, and other rideshare options, owning that second car is less important.

I had a good friend pass away, but towards the end of his life, he was in a financial hardship, as he was off work due to illness. My friend always purchased new cars about every three years, or more frequently, when a new design came out. I always asked myself, what if Larry had skipped the purchase of just one of those cars and invested it? If you skip one car, a $50,000.00 purchase, and invest it in yourself, that one-time $50,000.00 investment at 13.5% compounded annually will give you $177,389.79 in 10 years. The 50K car is now worth about $3,500 in 10 years. Would you rather have $177,389.79, or $3,500 in 10 years? You decide.

Selling Dreams

According to *Urban Dictionary*, Selling Dreams is "The act of promising with no intent to act on it, or also to intentionally deceive." As economic times get harder and harder, selling dreams become more frequent. The Dream Sellers often target already economically challenged individuals who cannot afford a setback or financial loss. You see people selling dreams all the time on social media. Selling dreams are here to stay for two reasons, first, there appears to be an endless supply of people to sell dreams to, and this creates the demand. The second major factor is there is an endless supply of dreams. Basic supply and demand. Remember this key fact: if it sounds too good to be true, then it probably is not true. In the history of time, there has not been one successful pyramid scheme. The only way to attain financial stability is sound financial principles coupled with investing and time. You never get something for nothing. If you have been sold a dream before, don't let it happen again!

You Are What You Spend Your Money On

You lend your resources according to your priorities. What's important to you is a good indicator of who you are. For example, a father spends his money on his children, because that is his priority, and that's what makes him a father, and the same goes for a mother. You can't be considered an investor without dedicating your resources to investments. If you spend your money on a lot of vanity objects, like clothes and jewelry, then you are most likely vain. A person who spends most of his or her money on drugs shows where their true priorities are, and so on. You don't have to look in the mirror to determine who you are, but a review of your face will give a pretty accurate picture. I need you to figure out who you are, and decide who you want to be. Be very aware of where you lend your resources, because that has a direct correlation of who you are, and where you are heading. Your goal is to be a millionaire, so make sure you are not over-dedicating your resources on things that are not helping you meet your seven year goal.

It's Not About Making Money, It's About Building Wealth

Making money only takes care of today, however wealth takes care of today and tomorrow. In my faith, the scripture says, "In every life, some rain shall fall," so with that being said, everyone will have a rainy day. You need to be prepared for it. The only way to prepare for a financial "rainy day" is by building wealth, so when the rainy day comes, you have a dry shelter. Think of how different that rainy day would be if you had nowhere to go, it was cold, and your only choice was to stand outside in it. Or, you could have a nice dry, warm home with a fireplace, movies, and your favorite food. By building wealth, you are building your shelter.

Without wealth, financial hardships are setbacks. Financial setbacks are difficult, and take a long time to recover from. That recovery time limits you from living an abundant life, and remember that you only have one ride on this life roller-coaster, so you have to make the best of it. Financial recovery time is magnified as we get older, and the saddest financial counseling sessions are with seniors that are going through financial hardships. Working in my church funerals were very stressful financially, even though the congregation appeared affluent, several people passed away without life insurance. The burden would fall on the family. Often times, if the parents are struggling financially, then the kids are struggling financially. It is an unpleasant feeling to have an entire family in your office. They are as a group, struggling to put together a few thousand dollars to have a decent funeral service for their family member. Financial instability is one strong gene that is passed down from generation to generation. Somebody has to make a change.

When you are actively wealth building, the money you make today takes care of you tomorrow. Can you see the money you earned over the past 5 years, or even 10 years? If not, you are not building wealth, you are just surviving. Wealth is power. You have more choices in life when you have a reasonable measure of wealth. In this country, many individuals go without the basics needs in life because of finances like healthcare or dental care. Imagine having a toothache for weeks, because you can't afford the dental visit. Also, in this country, women have accepted unwanted harassment at work due to their financial situation.

Wealth is security and peace of mind, and there are consequences of not building wealth. Think of the squirrel story you learned as a child, where one squirrel gathered nuts for the winter, while another squirrel just chilled and ate all the nuts he found. Well, it's now November in Chicago, do you have any nuts?

No Chapter 7

Chapter 7 means bankruptcy, and *The Millionaire Maker* doesn't create bankrupt people, I makes millionaires! Chapter 7 is not some magical word like "Abra Kadabra." A magician says this before a trick, and many people thinks it's a magical reset button. A chapter 7 bankruptcy has serious consequences, even though chapter 7 is the most common bankruptcy filed in the United States. Chapter 7 involves the courts assigning a trustee and liquidating your assets to satisfy your debts. In other words, the courts takes your stuff, sells it off to the highest bidder, and that pays your bills. That is not cool. They comb through your personal affairs with a fine tooth comb, and usually it does not end the way you intended. I understand in extreme cases some form of bankruptcy is unavoidable. However, it should be entered very carefully. I recommend exploring all other options: credit counseling, direct negotiation with creditors, and selling unnecessary items, before considering a chapter 7.

Chapter 8: Money Management for Millennials

Overview

- College graduates financial checklist.
- Investing for the younger generation.

I attended my nephew's college graduation ceremony from one of the most prestigious colleges in America. Seeing him in his cap and gown was extremely rewarding. As we sat down for the celebratory lunch with his mom and dad, I told my own family members, "I would suggest taking this book with you to your next college graduates ceremony, or better yet, give it as a gift to the new graduate." Just think, if someone you respected gave you this exact same advice and coaching, how much better would your own financial situation be? Here are a few college graduate essentials for finance:

1. Start small, because time is on your side if you start investing early. Before you get your first paycheck, have the company automatically deduct 5% to go directly to your 401K. This prevents you from getting used to spending the money that you should be saving. You won't miss what you never had. When deciding on a job, ensure you don't just consider the salary. You must know the true value of a job and those are: benefits, stability, job satisfaction, and fit. Weigh all of those before selecting a permanent job, because the employer could entice new talent with a generous salary that masks a poor benefits package.

2. Know if the employer is willing to contribute to any matching funds in your 401K. For example, you receive 2 separate job offers. Job one is offering a 100K salary, with no 401K match, and average health benefits, until you reach a certain level, which could take a few years. Job number 2 is offering 90K salary with 10% matching funds after 90 days of employment, and excellent health benefits. Well, the no brainer should be job number 2 with the 90K salary, if you take full advantage of the benefits package. When selecting a job, do the math!

3. During the first day on the job, plan for the last day on the job. Even though a company may appear stable, economic times change rapidly. Never think that you always will have a job. Therefore, every payday, ask yourself this question, "What if this was my last check?" So, always have contingency plans in place (extra income generator and debt reduction plan).

4. Build a separate savings, and remember that your 401K is your main vehicle to retirement, so don't dip! Often, people make the critical mistake of using their 401K as their emergency plan, and that is not what it is for.

5. Negotiate student loan debt with new employer! You are fresh out of college, and most graduates leave with a mountain of debt. Many people fail to ask the potential new employer to bear some of that burden. Look at it this way, and feel free to summarize this in a pitch, you just spent 4 years of your life, and thousands of dollars, to exclusively use your knowledge and skills attained to benefit this company. It would be very reasonable for the employer to contribute 35% to your student loan debt as a signing bonus. Even the Federal Government assists with student loan debt, but the trick is, you must negotiate the amount before accepting the position. The offer is off the table immediately after acceptance. Continue education with your employer, if the employer offers tuition reimbursement. This could save you thousands in additional debt.

6. Take risks early! In any investing, the higher the risk, the higher the reward. If you make a mistake now, it will not kill you, because you will have plenty of time to recover. Therefore, take the risk now and move to safer investing as you build your portfolio.

7. Invest your pay increases from the start! For example, you receive a promotion at work resulting in a 5K per year increase. You must at least increase your 401K contribution by 2.5K. This method will get you well on your way, and you'll be retiring in your 30s.

8. Get a mentor. There is so much information within constructing a secure financial future, especially in the beginning. I suggest you receive a financial mentor who you can trust, and has demonstrated financial stability and success over the long haul. Therefore, you can learn from their experience and be even more successful.

9. Buy real-estate early. I repeat myself when it is important. Buy real-estate early. Don't you always hear the words, "I remember when they were giving those houses away over there, and now we can't even afford the neighborhood." Here is one simple easy million dollar move, so listen closely. Buy the cheapest, most run down property in the worst neighborhood that is closest to a major focal point, like the beach, downtown, or a lake. Chances are, fast forward 20 years of gentrification, it will be one of the smartest investments you ever made.

10. Track your progress and stay focused.

Kids Investing

I was sharing investment strategies with an associate who volunteers his time to work with children. He is very passionate about guiding them in the right direction. As the conversation ended and we were going on our separate ways, he called out to me and said that he wanted to ask me a very important question. He then asked, "At what age should I tell my kids they should be investing?" I replied, "As soon as they can pronounce the word investing."

Children are taught either good or bad financial habits. Unfortunately, studies show that 80% of children assume the financial identity of their parents or guardians, and only 20% either stratus up or down. So, if you want to help your children, then help yourself. Too many people in society, especially in poor communities, don't truly understand investing until later in life, when there is not a great deal of earning years left.

Children learn instinctively, and the best time to learn a language is during childhood. Children quickly master cell phones, computers, and other complex applications of social media. The number one reason children are not learning investment strategies is because

142

they are not exposed to it. Bad habits are hard to break, so are good habits. Investing should be a habitual behavior. The major factors of investing is money, rate of interest, and time. Of those three, time is the only factor that you can't get more of. Time is finite, and the only way to increase a finite factor is to start early. If you have a great deal of work to do in a day, and it all must be accomplished that day, then you get an early start and get ahead. That goes for finances also.

Consistent investing over a long period of time can be an effective strategy to accumulate wealth. Even small deposits to a savings account can add up over time. Let's say your child opens a lemonade stand at 10 years old and earns $1,000.00. He invests that money, and adds $100.00 per month to that investment, until he is 20. He will end up with a balance of $27,604.00, with a 12% annual rate of return. Now, I know you think that may not appear like a lot of money, but here is where the magic happens. If you save $1.00 per year, your savings will grow to $958,464.27 after 30 years, maintaining a 12% annual rate of return.

Grandparents, if you want to do the next generation a solid, teach your grandkids this lesson, and sew into their future. Create the first interest bearing trust fund in your families history. Parents, if you want to do your children a solid, teach your kids this lesson and assist them on staying on track. Teach them not to get sidetracked on material things that are only a temporary fad. Kids, if you want to do yourself a solid, then learn the story above. Also learn the principles of money and investing, and break the chain of living without the peace of mind of financial security. If you can pronounce the word investing, then you should be investing.

Millennial Millionaires

Millennials are the easiest group for me to coach to become millionaires, even though they are faced with unique challenges that previous generations did not face. My dad had one employer for 35 years who was never laid off, or forced out by a company merger. It is less likely now for a millennial to have that luxury. It is also unlikely for a millennial to desire to stay with one company for their whole career. In previous generations, their job was their main source of retirement income, as they earned a healthy pension upon retirement. This scenario is not impossible. However, it is unlikely and impractical because of the volatility of the job market. Therefore, I advise millennials to develop an "Outside Plan." This is a life financial plan where, from the first day employed, the main focus is on the last day employed. In the "Outside Plan," the millennial is the master of his or her own destiny, where they leverage time and technology to achieve a financially secure future.

The first component on the "Outside Plan" is to get a job, and be as consistent as possible in staying employed. The millennial should develop alternative income streams while they are employed, to flex during gaps in primary employment. A perfect example is Uber and Lyft drivers. Those occupations are easily transitioned into and out of. Consistent investing is critical to early success.

The second component is for the millennial to move up in the workforce, and invest a percentage of the increase. This principal is simple and effective. With every pay raise, the annual cost of living increases at least 50%, and is funneled into your IRA/401K. You are free to enjoy the remainder of the increase in your salary. This also prepares you for retirement living at a faster pace.

Keep debt low! Debt is a financial killer.

Start your 401k/IRA as soon as possible. Time works in your favor the earlier you start to invest. Remember that your IRA does not stand for "In Rainy

Affairs." Your IRA is not a rainy day fund, so don't dip into it unless it is the absolute last resort.

Purchase real-estate early, purchase your property in a low cost semi-trendy area, and play the waiting game. It would be even better to purchase in a few separate areas to increase your chances for sprawl and gentrification. This will multiply your investment several times over.

Finally, protect your growth with limited setbacks. Be careful entering into an emotional relationship with someone, until you understand their financial literacy. Don't be a co-signer or enter into joint ventures with individuals who have not been as prudent as you. Usually this dream situation turns out to be a nightmare for the person with the good credit.

Chapter 9: Draw Your Map to Your Million

Overview

- Your map is a visual aid for your plan to get to your goal of $1,000,000.

- Key components to your map.

- Use compound interest.

- Drawing your map helps you stay on track throughout your wealth-building journey.

Helpful tools for calculating. I drew my map to my first million after my mother passed away, and I decided that I was done with living hand-to-mouth. Yes, I lived H2M also, so I don't judge anyone. I deserved more, and not being financially secure was not for me. I was in a relationship at the time, and she was not fully on-board with the plan. I solicited her input in drawing out the map, however she was always a little too busy. After I developed the plan pretty much on my own, I shared it with her, looking for an excited reaction, because we were going to be millionaires in a few short years. I got a "that's nice" reaction. Nevertheless, I had the plan, and I knew it would work if we just stuck to it. Remember, numbers don't lie, people do. I gave her a copy and asked her to review it so we can discuss it over dinner the next day. I placed the copy of the map under her briefcase so when she left that next morning, she would grab it. I came home after work and saw the plan still sitting in the same place that I left it. I realized that I needed to get this train going before she was going to get aboard. So, that's what I did! I got a couple of side hustles and started executing my plan. Once she saw me buy my first property cash, complete the renovation, and then start making passive income from it as well, I had her full attention. So, if you are in a single situation, you don't have to convince anyone. However, if you are in a couples arrangement, then don't worry if the other person can't see the vision just yet. Just press forward and they will eventually come around.

I am going to include an actual map that I helped someone create as an example. Remember, every map is as unique as your own fingerprint, but I recommend every map to contain some key components. The key components every map should have are: real-estate, 401K, general savings, extra income, compounding factors, net worth tracking, clear annual goals, and finally, a finish line.

Real-estate Component

Real-estate component is a critical component no matter how you construct your plan, because you can use real-estate in several ways. Real-estate is one of the best methods to earn passive income through. Ownership and passive income, combined with compound interest, is the engine that propels you to your first million. This is usually a very safe investment, because there is only a limited supply of land, and space is becoming more and more a premium each year as the population grows. Real-estate is the method that most American millionaires have made their millions from, so it would only make sense to make it your base.

Finally, property ownership has an advantage over most investments, due to the fact you can actually see and put your hands on it. Also, with property ownership, you can make physical improvements and attain sweat equity. That is impossible within stock markets. I use real-estate heavily in my map to my million to generate my monthly passive income, as well as build my net worth simultaneously. Here is an actual example from one of my clients, I showed him a way to own seven rental properties free and clear. After taxes and insurance, he earned an average return of $800.00 per unit. That is $5,600.00 per month as monthly passive income.

401K Component

The 401K component's number one advantage is the tax deferment options. Take advantage of the full employer contributions. If you have the option of a 401K with employer matching of contributions, then invest the maximum you can to receive all employer matching funds available to you. If you invest 10% of your check, then the employer will match that percentage. If you don't take advantage of the full employer matching, then you are essentially leaving money on the table, and that is a no-no in your map to your million. Another great advantage is that it is semi-automatic. You can almost set it and forget it. However, you have to keep in mind market fluctuations, and how it affects your yield. Don't get overworked with daily watching, because this is a long-term endeavor.

Here is a 401K trick that I do, and I recommend everyone should as well. I start my 401k at 6% with an employee match at 5%. That is an 11% annual savings. If you use my method, compounded annually at 10%, you will end up with $15,539.00 in 7 years. That will provide you with a monthly income of $1,294.00. If you aggressively put at least 50% of all of your wage increases (salary/ yield dependent), then you can save up to $250,000.00 in 7 years. In turn, would yield you more monthly income.

General Savings Component

The General savings component is an extension of your 401K, and your general savings prevents you from going backwards on your journey to your first million. One of the most common financial mistakes I see pre-millionaires make, is not adequately building their general savings. I personally recommend this amount to be at least one-half of your salary. This is one of the key principles of this book. It is not enough just to have an adequately funded emergency fund, it also should be accompanied with an emergency financial plan. The emergency financial plan is the plan you develop in advance, while you are not stressed over a job loss or medical emergency. During those times, you may not have the time to call creditors, or think of everything that needs to be done. Make a list of all unnecessary spending, and eliminate them to build your savings.

Extra Income Component

The extra income component is that hustle money we discussed earlier. Remember, we are going for the snowball approach. Try to put all your extra income into your plan by either investing in real-estate, 401K, or general savings. Remember not to reward yourself too much with this money. Love your hustle, therefore you can sustain it and be the best at it. In a few short years, you may transition totally to your beloved hustle. Don't do anything that will jeopardize your family, or your future for extra income. Your plan will get you where you desire to be if you just work the plan and stay on course.

When plotting your map to your million, remember that there is no magical "three easy steps," or "my secret method." The best kept secret in finance is that there are no secrets. You'll hear a house flipper on the radio soliciting a few motivated people to come to the local hotel ballroom and sign-up for a "secret list," in addition to their "secret method." The same financial principals worked one thousand years ago, and will continue to work, with no secrets involved. Often times, those scams waste valuable time and resources. Remember, numbers don't lie, people do. Stick to the tried and true basics, like compound interest, The Rule of 72, and use online tools and apps that are available today.

At some point, you will pass the inevitable point when your passive income is earning enough for you to reach your million dollar goal, without personally contributing any more money. At this point, interest is working for you, and not against you. You are making money in your sleep now.

Income properties			General savings		401 K 15 K year		The business	
			7K yr.		YR 1	71 K	**Year**	**Goal**
YR 1	Property 1	$750.00	YR 1	10K	YR 2	94 K	YR 1	Website/cards, 3 cont., business credit card
YR 2	Property 2	$800.00	YR 2	17K	YR 3	120 K	YR 2	
YR 3	Property 3	$800.00	YR 3	24K	YR 4	148 K	YR 3	
YR 4	Property 4	$700.00	YR 4	31K	YR 5	179 K	YR 4	
			YR 5	38K	YR 6	214 K	YR 5	
Adjusted for expenses = $3,050.00 month			YR 6	45K	YR 7	252 K	To build residual through this	
			=585 per month		8% Return on 250k = 2K (mo.) @ 10% interest avg. $1,250 per month			

Year Goals

1. One property ($750 monthly rental)
2. Get to total $0.00. No debt + keep Honda (no matter what they say).
3. 401K at 71K.
4. General Savings at 10K.
5. The website, cards, three contacts, and business credit card.

Monthly Income		Net Worth	
Properties	$3,050.00	Property 1	80K
401K	$2,000.00	Property 2	100K
Themis	$1,500.00	Property 3	100K
	=6,550.00	Property 4	170K
		401K	252K
		Savings	50K
		The business	250K
Projected net worth in 20XX >>>>>		$1 million	

To develop your map. I am including one of several methods that I recommend, which is the (7 by 7) method. The (7 by 7) method is a tracking tool where you list seven sources of income, and then project the income from each source, until you get to seven years. Then, it is as simple as doing the math. It should add up to 1 million dollars, and if it doesn't, see what source could generate more income, and then adjust it. Also, identify your least productive source and replace it with another source. You must spend time developing this before you begin your process.

154

(7 by 7) Tracking Tool							
	Source1	Source 2	Source 3	Source 4	Source 5	Source 6	Source 7
Year 1							
Year 2							
Year 3							
Year 4							
Year 5							
Year 6							
Year 7							
Total							

I am going to give you a scenario that I advised a young couple a few years ago. I will also use actual data they provided on their financial counseling update session. Of the seven sources, I suggest three sources always be real-estate, 401K, and general savings, but if you don't have one of those three, use your imagination and tailor your plan to your unique situation.

Tom and Mary are a young married couple with 2 kids, and a total household income of 87K annually. That's about average for the American family household income. Both work, and Tom makes about 44K a year, while Mary brings home the rest of the bacon. They have extensive credit card debt and two car payments. They are operating in a deficit situation and going further and further in a hole of debt. After discussing their situation, I gave them some homework to do. This was the route they decided to take:

1. They had 12K in credit card debt, and they could only afford to pay the minimum. (This would have taken them 25 years to pay off at the rate they were going.)

Solution: Cash in Tom's 401K of 13K

(Savings) $525.00 per month

2. They had a Benz and a Beamer. I call that a "blunder."
   - They sold both cars and purchased a gently used car for the remainder of Tom's 401K, and minimal monthly payments
   - **Solution:** Sold both cars they had payments on, both were luxury name brand, with extremely high maintenance cost. This, in turn, lowered their insurance, gas, and operating cost.
   - **Savings:** $1,875.00 per month.

3. With their savings, they now can afford to live off one monthly salary, and invest the other.

Now, it's your turn to draw your map to your million.

Chapter 10: Check Your Course

Overview

- Your map is a visual aid for your plan of hitting your goal of $1,000,000.

- Drawing your map helps you stay on track throughout your wealth-building journey.

After I drew my map to my first million, I was married with a two income household. All of my accounts appeared very wealthy, from the outside looking in. However, it was quite the opposite, I was drowning in debt and bills. A lot of money was coming in every month, and a lot was going out every month. I asked myself, "Where is all the money going?" At the time, my now my ex-wife was the bill payer, or check writer, so to speak. I asked her for a summary of all the bills and debts. As she explained the bills to me, I was unable to make sense of it all. I couldn't wrap my head around, and I had a feeling that she couldn't either. So, I had to simplify it as much as possible to get a real understanding. Remember, the first step I teach is to make a decision. I had my mind made up, and this would not be my future of living from paycheck to paycheck. Don't get me wrong, I liked my lifestyle, and I was willing to do whatever it required to increase my means, so I could live the lifestyle I desired.

Don't over complicate your map. My theme was "little by little," I was going to crawl out of debt. Getting out of debt is the second principal step in the process of "getting to zero," because if you're in debt, then you start every month in the negatives.

Breaking Goals Down

Each goal that we create for ourselves can usually be broken down. For instance, if the goal is to clean your car, then that may entail washing the exterior of the car, cleaning all four of the tires, waxing, vacuuming the interior seats and floor, getting rid of any trash inside the car, and wiping the interior surfaces down with an upholstery protectant. If we focus on doing each of these smaller tasks, then we eventually achieve our goal of having cleaned our car.

Your financial goals really aren't any different. There are baby steps that you have to take before you can make the leap to obtaining your million, and being a stable millionaire. Throughout this book, I've shared with you what those steps are and how to complete them. If you follow along as I'm describing, then you will find yourself entering the Millionaire's Club before you know it!

Protecting Your Commitment

Protect your commitment so you don't let it slip your mind--trust me, it's possible under the right circumstances. Here are some ways that you can safeguard your millionaire goal, and make sure it remains your central focus at all times.

Ditch the Dream Killers

As I told you earlier, Dream Killers are to be avoided as much as possible. If you find yourself regularly running into people who can't, or won't, support your dreams, then do what you can to distance yourself from them. I don't mean to downplay how difficult this can be if you have a Dream Killer in your life whom you have known for a long time. Dream Killers come in all shapes and sizes, from all walks of life. That means that anybody-- from your supervisor, to your barber, or even your spouse (remember my story about me and my ex-wife) could be a Dream Killer. I hope to help you understand that if you have strong suspicions that someone close to you is a Dream Killer, then don't think they aren't trying to sabotage you just because you are in love with them. You've known them for a long time, or they gave birth to you, but sometimes love does not matter. These are the most challenging kinds of relationships to disengage from. However, if they are Dream Killers, then you must limit your contact with them.

Stepping Aside

Getting Dream Killers out of your life doesn't always mean having some major confrontation with them or a long, drawn-out discussion about seeing or talking to each other less often (or not at all). More often than not, we end up working to keep these people in our lives, and we don't even realize it. Therefore, keeping them out of our regular social circle is actually easy, and often a relief. Our lives become less chaotic, less tense, and more enjoyable when these energy-sapping people are no longer a part of our daily routine.

For example, if one of your close friends is someone you have identified as a Dream Killer, then you can call them once each week, instead of every day. Or maybe you could have dinner with them once each month, instead of a few times each week. You can let them know that you're busy, need some alone time, or have started a new relationship (you don't have to tell that it's a new relationship with money). You also have the option of being open and honest with them about why you are distancing yourself from them. You can let them know that they are negative, they make fun of you, or they belittle you every time you attempt something positive. However, if you go this route, you need to be prepared for three types of scenarios that may take place.

First, they may hear you. Though this event isn't very likely, it is possible. Maybe they never realized how you felt about comments they made about your hopes and dreams. If this is the case, they will likely feel guilty, and thank you for being honest with them about your feelings. They'll also make an effort to better themselves within your friendship in the future. If this happens, you must consider yourself ultra-blessed, because the following two scenarios are usually what happens when someone is confronted about their off-putting, habitual behavior.

The second option is that they will become defensive and offended that you would bring their behavior to their attention. Especially if it may sound like you're blaming them for any problems in the friendship. They may try to argue, though there's no need for you to contribute to that scene by responding. The upside is, you will definitely be getting that distance you were looking for. They may work through their anger over time, and maybe you can eventually resume your friendship after you've reached your goal, but they will likely want to be separated from you for a while.

The third option is that they will "break-up" with you. They will decide that they are so indignant about what you have told them that they don't want to be friends with you anymore. While this can be painful, often it is for the best. This means you have likely simply dodged a bullet.

Leaving the Leeches

The same goes for friends and family who have asked you to give them money in the past. Once you stop trying to shoulder other people's financial responsibilities and focus on your own, it's smarter for you to decline their requests.

This can be difficult at first, especially if you share a really close relationship with someone who regularly begs you for money. You may even feel guilty about saying no to them. But, what people usually find out when they start saying no, and sticking to that no, is that they get asked much less often over time.

One reason for this is because people find out that you are no longer behaving like an ATM. Knowing this, they simply don't bother asking you, because they know what your answer will be. Another reason is, the people who you considered "friends" will slowly gravitate towards other people who are still willing to give them money when they ask for it. This means, they're no longer hanging around you and regularly trying to get money out of you.

Once you ditch the Dream Killers and leave the Leeches behind, you will find that you have created a cleaner, calmer daily life for yourself, with fewer people nipping at your wallet. At the same time, your quality of life goes up, because you don't have to spend so much of your time anticipating when money is going to somehow come up within a casual conversation.

Assess as You Go

Checking your course is not a one-time event. Just like with any long-term project, it's helpful to check in and make sure that you are headed in the right direction, and have everything you need in order to be successful. Once you have your map drawn up, you can choose a particular day of each month to check your progress. It could be your second payday, the middle of the month, or maybe even the first of each month. Mark it down on your paper calendars and make sure that there is a reminder in your phone. Ask yourself the following questions each time you stop to check your course, so that you can make sure you will successfully reach your goal:

Where was I this time last month?

Consider the speed at which you are progressing, and evaluate whether or not it is enough to meet your goal on the due date you specified. Think about whether you have stepped closer, or farther away from your goal. This helps you understand if you can maintain the course at your given rate, or if you need to pick up the pace a little bit, in order to get back on schedule.

What did I do last month that worked for me?

If anything happened that was helpful, then figure out ways to incorporate it into your daily routine. If it helped you earn extra money, then don't let it be a fluke. Let it work for you over and over again. These could be things like picking up an extra shift or two at work, surprisingly getting a long-lost loan repaid from someone who owed you money, or getting paid for volunteering to help someone out (with a move, their homework, a small repair, etc.).

What did I do last month that I need to try to avoid in the future?

If something hurt your progress, then figure out ways to keep it from happening again. These could be things such as accidentally leaving money at an ATM, breaking something costly that needed to be replaced, or suffering from overdraft charges at your bank.

What events are coming up next month that I need to prepare to deal with?

Taking a moment to think about what's coming next gives you time to prepare. This could include birthdays (buying gifts), less-than-monthly bills (water bills, P. O. Box rental fee), or holidays (outings, local festivals, etc.).

Be vigilant about where you are on your journey, and you will likely end it successfully. Keeping these guidelines in mind, you can make your road to your first million a faster and smoother one.

Develop a Reasonable Budget and Stick to It

The number one budget buster is developing your budget to fail, by setting unreasonable goals, and being too restrictive. You will feel urgency and aggressiveness, and that's great, because you will need both of those attributes to be successful in your journey. However, put some easy wins in your plan to encourage, maintain, and stick to the plan.

Make Your Map Clear

If your plan is too vague, then it is hard to keep track of your progress, and you will lose focus. Believe it or not, most people forget their daily tasks if they don't have a list.

Update Your Map to Show Progress

Keeping track of your progress will encourage you to keep going, also. Remember to get rich slowly. Slow and steady gets it done. Review expensive habits and minimize them. It is good to reward yourself within reason.

Develop Checkpoints in Your Plan

This helps you review your plan. Give your plan a thorough review, and determine if any adjustments are needed. This is an opportunity to get more aggressive and creative. That's why it is important to make your goals achievable in the beginning. Also, all goals should be SMART goals.

SMART goals is a concept developed by George Doran in 1981. It was originally presented to the world in an article he co-wrote and published, as a way for businesses to strategize more effectively. For example, things like meeting financial goals, or creating marketing campaigns. SMART goals are now used in a wide variety of disciplines. Even fields like psychotherapy use SMART goals. It helps develop treatment plans for people suffering from various mental health diseases. Such as, drug addiction or schizophrenia. For our purposes, we're going to take SMART goals back to their business roots and apply them to the business of getting our first million dollars.

Specific

Be precise and clear about each of your goals. *I will be rich*, is a vague goal. The word "rich" has a different definition for every person. It depends on what kind of money they currently make, how much debt they are in at any given time, what their relationship with money has been like throughout their lives, and what culture or country they happen to have been born into.

However, something like *I will become a millionaire* is a little bit more specific. You have just narrowed in on your target amount of money. We can crank up the specificity a little further with a goal like *I want to have a net worth of $2,000,000, with $1,000,000 liquid cash in my savings account.* Now that's a 20/20 vision!

As we discussed earlier, it is helpful to speak positively and frequently about our goals, and the financial vision we have for ourselves. This helps keep us motivated and focused on making sure it happens. When we can be specific, that helps out even more, because we carve with our words a more exact image of our financial future. Instead of some vague blob that may or may not be better than the situation we find ourselves in at the moment.

As you start planning your financial goals, you can begin with vague ones and tighten them up.

Measurable

Making sure that a goal is measurable just means making sure you have a way to clock your progress. Measurability includes outlining when you know you have met said goal, so that you know when you are making progress towards that goal. It's just as important if you are *not* making progress. This helps you figure out what isn't working for you, so that you can stop doing that, and adopt other tactics instead.

For example, a way of measuring financial progress may be you keep track of the current balance, or amount of total deposits on your bank statement each month. If your goal is to maintain $5,000 or more in deposits for six consecutive months, then it will be easy to track that goal, because you specified what you are going to measure (the amount of the total deposits to the account for the month). If you notice that one month you only deposited $4,000, you can review the account summary to figure out why you're $1,000 short of your deposit goal for that particular month.

Achievable

This may seem obvious to some, but it can be difficult because of how honest you must be with yourself about your financial situation. Also, because we live in a "microwave culture," where we value things being done quickly, regardless of whether or not they are done well, it can be easy to slip into believing that the faster we get our millionaire statue, the better.

If a goal is achievable, that just means it can be accomplished with a reasonable and realistic amount of effort. So, maybe you're five-foot-two, two hundred pounds, and you only have one foot. You could set a goal saying that you are going to be a three-time NBA all-star within five years. However, given your physical circumstances, that is highly unlikely and therefore would not be considered "Achievable" for our purposes. Technically, it may be physically possible for you to bribe, blackmail, or intimidate everyone that you need to in order to make it onto a professional team, but you can't keep every opposing team from scoring. It's unrealistic to believe the other team will wait patiently while your teammates hoist you up so you can score points.

However, even if you were somehow partially successful, this is a convoluted, wildly unreasonable, and very unlikely feat for you to accomplish. So, when you're putting together your SMART goal, remember to be realistic when considering your options and circumstances.

Relevant

Stay focused on what your needs are in your life. Make sure every step you take puts you a little bit closer to accomplishing your dreams. There is no need for you to have a SMART goal for every component and aspect of your life. This is overwhelming and doesn't help you. If your mind and energies are spent in a hundred different places, then you're unlikely to make any progress at all on even one of your goals (unless one of them was to drive yourself insane). For the purposes of this book, of course, we are focused on becoming millionaires within approximately seven years. Make sure your SMART goals stay within this realm. Once you've achieved your millionaire status, feel free to apply SMART goals to other aspects of your life. Such as academics, romance, parenting, or physical health.

Time Limited

It is critical that you give yourself a due date for your goals. You don't have to be completely inflexible about it, but try and stick to the time frame you set when you created the goal. If extreme circumstances take place, such as the death of a loved one, or the loss of a job, then the date can be adjusted to compensate for the delay. Will you get it done tomorrow, next week, next year, or ten years from now? Having a due date on a goal allows you to assess your progress and speed. Due dates are also a great way to hold yourself accountable for getting goal-related tasks completed on time.

SMART Goal:
Putting it all together.

So, now that we've walked through all the components of a SMART goal, let's examine a few examples of how a completed SMART goal might look.

Not so smart goal: I will be a good student.
SMART goal: I will maintain a 3.8 grade point average for three consecutive semesters by the end of 2020.

Not so smart goal: I will be a famous writer.
SMART goal: By 2020, I will be on the New York Times bestseller list four times.

Not so smart goal: I will be rich.
SMART goal: I will have a net worth of $500,000, and have no outstanding debt by January 1st of 2028.

Review your map daily. This keeps your plan on the front of your mind. Often times, we forget the commitment that we made to ourselves and family.

Call your creditors monthly, or even weekly. Communication is the key to everything. Try to develop a relationship with your creditors, and inform them of your goal. You may be surprised by how helpful they can be. In all cases, when you call your creditors, make sure you do what you say you are going to do. The more they see that you keep your word, the more flexible they will become.

Unique Challenges to Couples

According to a study by SunTrust Bank, money issues are also responsible for 22% of all divorces, making it the third leading cause. Everyone wants to feel secure, and money is a wonder drug for feeling secure! Finances should be discussed prior to getting serious in your relationship. Understand your potential mate's life priorities, because that is the number one factor that determines spending priorities. If a gentleman loves sports and cars, then he is more likely to spend more on sporting events and automobiles. If a young lady likes fashion and cosmetics, she is more likely to spend more on clothes, shoes and accessories. Unfortunately, our frivolous priorities are usually not on more productive things, like house cleaning and yard maintenance. However, they are what they are. It is important to pre-establish spending limits on these things before entering into a union, because it is proven to be more difficult to negotiate after.

Tim's Tips for Couples

1. Know your partners financial perception before taking the plunge.
2. Clear up as much separately accumulated debt before getting serious.
3. Be very truthful of your situation, and allow access to joint accounts.
4. Read common financial literature. I suggest *Your Map to your Million*, I heard the author is great.
5. Write a common vision to keep everyone on the same page.
6. Have financial rules that will never be crossed.
7. Have some individual spending money. A no questions asked, within reason, spending money.
8. Set business meetings up with your mate. Fellas, this could end real good or real bad, but everyone loves a good happy ending.
9. Be a team! If the quarterback of an NFL team throws an interception, then his teammates return to the huddle, encourage him, and then they run another play! As with finances, your partner/ your teammate

will make financial mistakes. Just huddle up, talk about the mistake, then keep pressing forward.

10. Communicate, communicate, and communicate! You can over communicate when it comes to feelings, but you can't over communicate when it comes to finances.

If you are truly in love, then your love is unlimited. However, your finances are very limited.

Chapter 11: Have a Finish Line

Photo Credit: Pexels

Overview

- It's important to create your own "finish line."
- Don't let progress become your nemesis.
- You don't have to ever beg, borrow, or steal to survive.
- Your "New Birthday" is when you attain your goal, because you haven't lived until you are financially free.

In the last chapter, we talked about how easy it can be to get caught up in the high of achieving your financial goals. That's why it's so important to create your own "finish line" when you create your map. If you keep in mind that, no matter how close you get to the finish line, you haven't yet crossed it, then you may be less likely to get sidetracked by your own accomplishments thus far.

If you get distracted by the prospect of making increasing amounts of money, then your progress can actually become your nemesis. Pre-millionaires often want to show off to themselves and other people once they start accumulating large amounts of money. They think they need a new car, thirty new outfits, or even some bling. However, as you start to pull away from $0.00 and up into the hundreds of thousands of dollars, you are truly starting to grow your wealth. Meaning, this is actually the worst time to be spending large amounts of money, especially frivolously. Now is not the time for instant gratification simply because you have the resources to purchase things that you may have been craving after for a long time. Now is the time to focus and stay on course.

Obtaining a realistic picture of your financial situation was a goal, and you achieved it! Getting out of debt was a goal, and you achieved it! Gaining a positive net worth so that you could start creating wealth was a goal, and you achieved it! Don't treat your million-dollar goal like a red-headed step child just because your bank account isn't overdrawn anymore. Remember how far you have come, and don't disrespect that hustling you did to get here. Build upon the hard work that you have done so that you can get closer to your ultimate goal: behaving in a habitually financially responsible manner. Also, obtaining your first million is just a bonus.

Even though I don't want you to go wild when you start building wealth, it's okay to recognize and celebrate your progress. I understand that you're delighted and proud of all that you have done. I call this point your "New Birthday." That's because you haven't really lived until you are financially stable, and have resources for the rest of your life. No more worries about where your next meal is coming from, who is going to pay the water bill, whether that strange number calling you is a bill collector or a job opportunity, or how you're going to get money for gas when you have $0.37 left in your checking account. Imagine walking into work with a new pep in your step because you are cloaked in a new confidence. This confidence comes from the *fact*-- not 'hope,' not 'belief,' not 'desire,' nor 'vision,'--that you could walk out the door and never look back and be *perfectly fine*. You no longer need the job, you're simply using the job to help you reach a long-term goal. When that burden of 'need' is lifted from your shoulders, you can behave like the calm, confident person you've always wanted to be. You've reached a special kind of freedom that very few people in the world ever come close to experiencing. And the people around you will notice the difference, too. Especially those who were consistently negative towards you, or who were always ready to negatively engage with you. When you're confident in yourself, it is much easier to let the things that people say about you roll off your back, instead of getting hooked into their nonsense by arguing with them, becoming defensive about a topic, or feeling guilty because you didn't give them pieces of your success-- especially when you haven't even actually reached your goal yet! This creates an opportunity for less stress in your romantic, familial, social, and professional relationships. You'll have no need to be jealous or resentful because of what someone else has. You can stop feeling sorry for yourself, because you have got your act together, and got your finances back on track. You don't have to ever beg, borrow, or steal to survive. This "New Birthday" should be commemorated with people who are very close to you that you trust (Dream Killers, exit stage left). This is NOT a make it rain party, or to brag or boast, but to be thankful and inspire others.

Seeing others be successful often inspires others to be successful, if they have a good heart. Share your strategies that worked for you and tell them about the book that started it all: *Your Map to Your Million.*

Unfortunately, for those who let their success overwhelm them, they will never get to experience this "New Birthday." If you don't stick to the basic principles that you achieved success with, then your financial fortitude will crumble in a matter of months, weeks, or maybe even mere days. Again, think back to all the star athletes, actors/ actresses, and musicians who seemed to have millions, and then fell destitute soon after. This is because achieving and maintaining wealth involves attitude and a mindset, coupled with an action plan. People who allow their progress to throw them off track, will buy video game consoles and tablets for their kids, or expensive meals at high-end restaurants a few nights each week, instead of waiting for special occasions a few times each year. They will insist on upgrading their cars, cell phones, or cable plans. Falling victim to retail therapy will make you squander everything you have worked so hard for. Retail therapy is worse than street drugs, because it is unquenchable.

So, I beg of you, please delay your gratification. I understand that there is an urge to "catch up" with all the material things and experiences that we have been wanting all our lives. I'm going to ask you to trust me when I tell you that there will come a time when you will be able to do all of those things without undoing all of your precious progress. Remember, you are seeking financial peace of mind, and financial peace of mind is priceless.

Chapter 12: Good Habits to Make, Bad Habits to Break, and Advice to Take

Overview

- My financial tips and quotes
- Financial habits to make
- Financial habits to break
- Key principles
- Helpful resources

Money is Funny, It Comes and Goes

Think of money like this: there is only a limited amount of it in circulation, and some people are getting more of it, while others are getting less of it. The tug of war is continuous. The people who are getting more of the money that is in circulation have a set strategy that has a proven track record of success. People with money have more power to get more money, because it is (somewhat) true that it does take money to make money. The reason that I say it is somewhat true is because ideas in action are a great means of making money. However, the idea must be accompanied by action to have earning potential. Also, the people who are getting more money also leverage ownership, and with ownership comes authority. Authority allows you to apply tolls for usage, therefore generating passive income. Lastly, the people piling more money in their coffers are lenders. Lenders are the controllers and owners of money. Therefore, they can apply a toll for usage.

On the contrast, the people who are getting less of that limited amount of money are the exact opposite. They are not operating on a proven financial plan. Therefore, in finances, strategy and awareness is everything. If you are unaware, and not executing your map to your million, you are losing.

Tim's Quotes

"Numbers don't lie, people do."

"One day you will run out of someday's."

"Aggressively investing in your future is not expensive, it's priceless."

"Financial peace of mind is priceless."

"You can never borrow your way to financial freedom."

"If you don't know where your money went in life, then you don't know where you are going."

"Every paycheck invokes choices that will decide the rest of your life. Choose wisely."

"Be the lender, and not the borrower." - Jesus

Tim's Tips

Ecclesiastes 7:12 "Wisdom is a shelter as money is a shelter, but the advantage of knowledge is this: Wisdom preserves those who have it."

Ecclesiastes 10:19 "A feast is made for laughter, and wine maketh merry: but money answereth all things."

Numbers are predictable, because 1 plus 1 will always equal 2. Therefore, learn the predictability of numbers and you will master it, instead of chasing it.

Take care of your own financial health first before you help someone else, that is not being selfish, but wise.

Never co-sign for anyone, because there is a reason that they need a cosigner, and you are soon to find out why.

Family and finances are very volatile. Never lend money to family members, but give what you can afford, with no repayment expected.

Financial Habits to Make

Focus on specific financial goals.

Pay bills ahead of schedule.

Monitor your credit report for accuracy.

Call your creditors and service providers quarterly, and negotiate a better deal.

Avoid debt.

Avoid spendthrift friends.

Seek expert advice.

Create a saving habit.

Make an investment goal amount each year.

Shop in GW Fashion: AKA Goodwill (No shame).

Financial Habits to Break

Stop spending more than you make.

Stop paying your bills at the last possible second.

Stop paying credit card minimums.

Stop attaining more credit.

Stop falling for get rich quick schemes.

Stop expensive habits.

Stop shopping at expensive stores.

Stop ignoring or deferring loan payment.

Stop buying expensive gifts (instead, make something

that is more personal).

Key Principles

- Persistence is key to healthy finances.
- Net worth = (Cash + Assets) – Debts.
- Contact everyone you owe money to at least every quarter, in order to negotiate more favorable terms for you (lower interest rate, lower payments, more manageable payment methods for you, etc.).
- Interest works against you in a bad way if you are in debt, or borrowing money.
- The more sources of income that you establish, the less dependent you become on one single source.
- Passive income is key. You want to get away from trading time on the clock for money. There are not enough hours in the day.
- Gentrification is very real and does not come and go. It doesn't stop and start. It is a continuous process, so always be alert.

- If it sounds too good to be true, then it probably is. In the history of time, there has not been one successful pyramid scheme.

- Financial get rich quick schemes are not worth destroying your reputation within your community, and even family.

- The only way to attain financial stability is sound financial principles, coupled with investing and time.

- The key components every map should have are: real-estate, 401K, general savings, extra income, compounding factors, net worth tracking, clear annual goals, and finally, a finish line.

- It is not enough to just have an adequately funded emergency fund. It should also be accompanied with an emergency financial plan.

- Strategic communication is the key to everything in finances.

- Stop complaining about how you don't make enough money. The truth is, you are not managing it well enough.

- **The rule of 72** is a shortcut to estimate the number of years required to double your money at a given annual rate of return. **The rule** states that you divide the rate, expressed as a percentage, into **72**. Years required to double investment = **72** ÷ compound annual interest rate.

- Double your money every day for 31 days starting with only one penny, you would have over 10 million on day 31.

Biography

Tim Jernigan, "The Millionaire Maker," is a retired United States Navy veteran and radio host. He is known as a finance and real-estate guru who takes a strategic approach to building wealth. Jernigan believes anyone can get out of debt, and go from $0.00, to one million, in 7 years.

Your million is in your mind!

Works Cited

1. Martin, Gary. "The Meaning and Origin of the Expression: Rule of Thumb." *Phrases.org.uk.* www.phrases.org.uk/meanings/rule-of-thumb.html.

2. Segal, Troy. "Compound Interest." *Investopedia.* investopedia.com/terms/c/compoundinterest.asp.

3. "What is a Smart Goal?" SmartGoalsGuide.com.

4. www.smart-goals-guide.com/smart-goal.html

MAP TO YOUR MILLION

www.ingramcontent.com/pod-product-compliance
Lightning Source LLC
Chambersburg PA
CBHW060554200326
41521CB00007B/572